Rob + Krystal,
welcome to small
Group Study!
9/28/10

CAPSIZED:

Finding Faith in Sinking Ships

Joseph P. Infranco

PublishAmerica
Baltimore

First printing

PublishAmerica has allowed this work to remain exactly as the author intended, verbatim, without editorial input.

Hardcover 978-1-4512-1961-6
Softcover 978-1-4512-1986-9
PAperback 978-1-4512-5440-2
Hardback 978-1-4512-6556-9
PUBLISHED BY PUBLISHAMERICA, LLLP
www.publishamerica.com
Baltimore

Printed in the United States of America

Dedicated to Valerie—my wife, best friend and partner in the journey of faith.
—Proverbs 18:22

Whenever I find myself growing grim about the mouth; whenever it is a damp, drizzly November in my soul … then, I account it high time to get to sea as soon as I can… If they but knew it, almost all men in their degree, some time or other, cherish very nearly the same feelings towards the ocean with me.

—*Moby Dick*

Table of Contents

Acknowledgements

I would like to acknowledge the input and suggestions of several friends. Doug and Christi Napier, both graduates of Dallas Theological Seminary offered valuable insights and editing tips. Thanks also to Pastor Mark Yule and Brett Harvey for their comments and helpful critiques. A special acknowledgement goes to my close friend, Ron Simmons, who pushed and inspired as needed. Special thanks also go to Professor Wayne Grudem, PhD, Research Professor of Theology and Biblical Studies at Phoenix Seminary, who reviewed the book concept and opening chapters and expressed his appreciation for the spiritual applications. Finally, thanks to my old friend Michael Brown, PhD, President and founder of ICN Ministries, who affirmed the concept and approved of Greek applications.

Preface to Capsized!

Back in the mid-sixties my brother and I huddled before our small television to watch an eminently forgettable series called "The Time Tunnel." While the details are fuzzy, I recall the gist of the sitcom; a few hapless time travelers in a "time machine" were propelled into the past, though they had no idea where and when the machine would transport them. Unlike H.G. Wells' time machine, they had no controls—and had to brave the machine's random whimsy. By fortunate coincidence for the viewer, they were usually propelled into dangerous and exciting adventures.

In one episode, the adventurers were whisked away by the machine and found themselves on the deck of a large passenger ship. They were momentarily relieved; here, at last, was an unthreatening destination. Who wouldn't like a nice ocean cruise? Things seem to have worked out well for once—until the camera panned on a life preserver that said: "S.S. Titanic." If the time visitors wanted a relaxing cruise, they were on the wrong boat.

Life is full of boats that are best avoided. But even when we realize we're in the wrong boat, getting *out* is generally more difficult than getting *in*. Depending on where you are, options may be very limited. A friend told me about an all day fishing trip he once took in Hawaii. The boat left very early to travel hours for a long day of fishing in prime waters. One man on the boat got terribly seasick, and there were no remedies on hand. He pleaded with the captain to return to port, but the captain replied he could not. There was a boat full of paying customers who wanted to fish. The seasick man then offered to refund the cost to every customer if the boat would turn back, but again—no deal. The customers wanted to fish, and were not interested in refunds. The seasick man curled up on the deck and lay there moaning, hoping to arouse sympathy—still to no avail. Finally the desperate passenger offered to *buy the boat* from the captain, who politely refused. Nothing could alter the unfortunate man's fate once he got in the boat.

This is a book about boats, both literal and figurative. For each topic I have selected a boat disaster from history (with apologies to those craft that are "ships") and placed it next to a Biblical account of a boat. There are many boats referred to in the Bible—more than you probably would guess. Jesus' earthly ministry in Galilee often involved boats; He traveled in them, taught from them, slept in them and worked miracles in and near them. These boats and the lives of the people who sometimes found themselves in the "wrong" boat become a metaphor for the human condition. There are boats called disobedience, discouragement, distraction, and so on. They are the familiar conditions that separate us from God. There are two significant questions for our lives on each boat: first, how did we get into it and the situation it represents? The second is perhaps more important—*how do we get out of a boat we should have never boarded in the first place?*

The lure of the sea, with all its romance and danger, is the setting for our look at boats—both from the Bible, and from some of the most notable tales of tragedy and inspiration known to humanity.

CHAPTER ONE: A BOAT CALLED DISTRESS

"I must confess that my imagination refuses to see any sort of submarine doing anything but suffocating its crew and floundering at sea."
H.G. Wells

Distress Under the sea

While a ship in distress can be terrifying under many circumstances, one of the most gripping histories of maritime disasters comes from the development of submarines. Submarine personnel are all too familiar with the dreaded concept of "crush depth." Through most of submarine history, subs were built to dive to a certain depth and no more. A disabled ship unable to control its movement might be doomed to sink slowly to the ocean floor. As it did so, the pressure of the ocean on the cabin built up unbearably to the point the sub's frame could no longer resist the outside pressure. There are stories of technicians at their monitoring equipment, listening helplessly, while a doomed ship glided downward until the dreaded popping noise of crush depth was heard. The death of a submarine, and the almost inevitable loss of all life aboard, has the nightmarish quality of a horror story.

One such story is the tragedy of the *USS Scorpion*, a 3,500-ton nuclear attack submarine that went missing in May, 1968. In a riveting account, told in the book *Blind Man's Bluff*, the authors tell of a military expert attempting reconstruction experiments to guess the ship's fate. The chapter "Death of a Submarine" describes the culmination of the simulated test:

"When (the) simulated turn was almost complete—maybe half a minute or so after he had called out 'right full rudder'—the staff called into the simulator: 'Explosion in the forward torpedo room.' The same information was fed into the computer, which began to register extensive flooding in the submarine. Fountain answered with a seemingly endless stream of orders: blow ballast, initiate watertight security, speed the boat. He did everything a submarine captain should do. Still, the mythical submarine continued to flood, and it continued to head toward the bottom. Exactly 90 seconds after Craven announced the explosion, it passed 2,000 feet—passed right through collapse depth—and the computer registered an implosion. Someone on the staff announced the event with one word: 'bang.'"

When the remains of the sub were found months later, the physical evidence supported the simulation, which events were likely caused by a bad battery on the ship. [1]

A Brief History of Submarines

Among the novelist Jules Verne's most fascinating science fiction is the story of the mysterious Captain Nemo and his submarine, the Nautilus. Published in 1870, decades before the beginning of the modern submarine age, the story told of an electric powered boat that roamed the seas, attacking ships from beneath the surface and battling fantastic and hideous sea creatures. The novel captured the imagination of many readers, but also scientists who dreamed that such a vessel was not far down the road.

The first designs for submarines actually go back centuries before Verne's novel. An Englishman named William Bourne designed a prototype submarine in 1578, but the first sub was not constructed until 1620. Early primitive submarines were used primarily for underwater exploration, though by the end of the seventeenth century the potential for military uses was being discussed, most notably for spy missions.

The idea of other military applications continued to develop through the eighteenth century. It is not commonly known that the first military submarine was used by the Continental Army during the Revolutionary War. The small egg shaped vessel, named *Turtle*, held a single man. It tried (unsuccessfully) to sink a British ship in New York Harbor, the only known attempt at military engagement during the war. By 1867, three years before Verne's novel about the Nautilus was published, a peroxide propulsion sub named the *Ictineo II* was built. The *Ictineo* was designed for a crew of two, and could dive to nearly 100 feet, though only for short runs of under two hours.

Submarines saw some limited use during WWI, though they were not a major part of warfare. The period between WWI and WWII brought dramatic technological advances, like sonar and improved breathing apparatuses, which would be critical to future use in warfare. According to the US Naval Academy website, submarine warfare really came into its own during WWII. The German U-Boat fleet nearly turned the tide of the war by cutting off supplies being shipped from America. On the other hand, the Academy's website claims that American-built subs were the critical factor for America's victory over Japan in the Pacific arena.

The end of WWII brought what is arguably the most significant development in the history of submarine warfare: the development of nuclear submarines. Again, according to the Academy's website, "(t)he development of nuclear power meant that a true submarine could finally be built. Free of dependence on the outside world, the submarine became a true underwater monster, prowling the deep in search of all traffic." Submarines became more efficient and silent, and capable of lightning quick devastating attack.

The first submarine to use nuclear energy in propulsion was an American ship, the USS Nautilus, named quixotically after Verne's ship in *Twenty Thousand Leagues Under the Sea*. It was, perhaps, recognition that technology had reached—or even surpassed—the science fiction of Verne's fertile imagination. With the advent of nuclear vessels, the age of the submarine was in full bloom, except no level of technology could insure that submarines were accident-proof. New technology created new benefits, but also new dangers. During the period of the Cold War, Russia lost at least four nuclear submarines due to technical failures, while many more suffered minor damage, radiation leaks and other issues. The United States lost two nuclear subs during this period, the *USS Thresher* and the *Scorpion*. The *Thresher* was destroyed by equipment failure; the *Scorpion* may have had equipment issues as well, but the exact cause of its loss is uncertain.

The following story chronicles a technical failure and a tragic accident in a Russian submarine called the *Kursk*. It is the story of a boat we could alternatively title "distress," whose fate was sealed by a government that fumbled and would not ask for outside help until it was too late.

The Kursk

The *Kursk* was no ordinary Russian submarine. As a National Public Radio report in 2003 noted, it was "(f)ast, stealthy and technologically complex" and "the pride of the cash-starved post-Soviet sea force." She was one of the largest, most powerful submarines in the world, with a surface displacement of almost

14,000 tons. The *Kursk*—the pride of the Russian force—was lost on August 12, 2000 in the Barents Sea, and its crew of 118 sailors perished. Although it was one of numerous recent maritime disasters, the *Kursk* stands out in one notable respect. It is remembered to this day as the Russian sub that refused outside help, or more precisely, the case in which the Russian government refused timely foreign assistance.

The setting for the tragedy was the Barents Sea, part of the Arctic Ocean north of the Scandinavian Peninsula and east of Greenland. While coursing through the frigid waters of the Barents, the *Kursk* was conducting routine military drills and firing dummy torpedoes at a Russian battlecruiser. Shortly after firing its torpedoes the *Kursk* was ripped by two successive explosions. The first, a chemical explosion, detonated with the force of as much as 500 pounds of TNT, and registered 2.2 on the Richter Scale. According to some accounts, the wounded submarine sank to a depth of 350 feet when a second and far more severe explosion tore through the sub with a force of 3-7 tons of TNT. The second blast occurred a little more than two minutes after the first, mortally crippling the sub and condemning its survivors to a watery grave unless help arrived quickly.

Spencer Dunmores gives the following account of the chaos immediately after the explosions:

"In a fraction of a second, a routine exercise had become a catastrophe. The Kursk's forward section disintegrated, flooding her torpedo compartment. The intricate maze of pipes and valves, gauges and controls that gave her life had been reduced to a tangle of scrap metal. In the forward compartments, every officer and crewman was dead, their lives snuffed out in the blink of an eye... (D)eath would have come quickly for crewmen in the reactor control rooms and the turbines, for the boat tipped, nose down, its steam turbines still delivering power until the automatic shutdown. .[2]

There is credible speculation that the first explosion, which was chemically induced, occurred when a crew member accidentally allowed a potassium superoxide cartridge to come in contact with water. These cartridges are used to absorb carbon dioxide and release oxygen to enable survival in critical situations. There is a twin irony to the deadly accident; first, a cartridge designed to sustain life caused the initial explosion. The second irony is that the numerous additional cartridges on board may have allowed the crew access to oxygen, and may have allowed some of the crew to survive for days, waiting for help that never arrived.

There has been much debate over the cause of the explosions, but the most gut-wrenching speculation has focused on the survivors in the rear of the ship. How long did these crewmen live before death by asphyxiation or other cause? American news stations following the story reported that sailors in the ship were communicating with Russian vessels on the surface by tapping messages in code, though there is no way to know whether the rapping noises actually came from the frantic crew or disintegrating equipment.

While Russian authorities publicly maintained that the crew likely died very quickly, notes on the body of Captain-Lieutenant Dimitry Kolesnikov show that 23 sailors (of the 118 aboard) survived in a compartment in the rear of the boat. According to BBC reports at the time portions of the note were released, Kolesnikov wrote: *"All the crew from the sixth, seventh and eighth compartments went over to the ninth. There are 23 people here. We made the decision because of the accident. None of us can get to the surface. I am writing blindly."* Kolesnikov also wrote a touching farewell note to his wife Olga, whom he had married only weeks earlier. Both messages, carefully wrapped in plastic and stuffed in his shirt, were retrieved after his death.

According to official accounts, the Russian Navy did not locate the stricken vessel until nearly sixteen hours after the accident. Once located at a depth of 354 feet, Russian authorities waited another fifteen hours before lowering the first rescue vessel. The following day, British and American authorities publicly offered assistance in the rescue effort. The offer was ignored for two full days, even though it was common knowledge that both the offering nations had more advanced technology than the struggling Russian military. Finally, days later, President Vladimir Putin instructed the Russian navy to accept any proffered offer of foreign help. It would take another three days before British and Norwegian ships arrived at the scene. Norwegian divers finally reached the *Kursk* on August 20, 8 days after the explosions; when the first hatch was opened, it was apparent there were no survivors.

After the stricken sub was recovered and a full investigation conducted, authorities released the story about the note found on the body of Captain-Lieutenant Kolesnikov. A New York Times report on the disclosure noted as follows:

"On Moscow streets this evening, Russians greeted the disclosure of the note with studied cynicism. 'I expected this. I think they took too long. They should have saved them,' said a 46-year-old civil servant who would be identified only as Galina. 'But who can you blame? Everything in our country has already collapsed.' "[8]

The story of the *Kursk's* destruction was eloquently told by British journalist Robert Moore in his book *A Time to Die*. In an interview with National Public Radio's Robert Siegel, Moore opined that the delay in accepting help minimized any chance of rescuing the trapped sailors. The Russian leadership's penchant for secrecy sealed the crew's fate. In an interview, Moore explained to Siegel "it was really a case of political paralysis."

The Cause of Political Paralysis

Moore is likely correct that the Russian government experienced a kind of political paralysis, but what lies beneath that diagnosis? Why would a government refuse help from other nations that might save the lives of a crew? What motives would lead to such a decision? One word that springs to mind is *pride*. A struggling nation did not want to admit its shortcomings or inadequacies and therefore preferred "secrecy." Maybe someone else could handle it more efficiently, but Kremlin leaders did not want to admit this in front of the world. The predictable result was the loss of all lives aboard the *Kursk*. Would it have made a difference if Russia had asked for help immediately? No one can know, though the odds certainly would have improved.

The paralysis of the Russian government is more common in human nature than we might want to admit. The desire to avoid looking weak or unable—pride, if you like—is subtle and shows itself in our lives in many forms. Usually the results are not as visibly catastrophic as the *Kursk*, except pride erodes our souls and separates us from God. The Bible makes the point continually and emphatically. If we exalt ourselves, Jesus says, we will be humbled; but if we humble ourselves, we will be exalted by God. Scripture even tells us that God resists the proud but gives grace to the humble. Humility—the polar opposite of pride—

sees and acknowledges vulnerability. Jesus called his disciples to cultivate this and even imitate Him in its pursuit: *come to me all who labor and are heavy laden and I will give you rest; take up your yoke and learn from me, for I am humble and lowly of heart. (Matthew 11:28-29)*

Imagine being one of those sailors for a moment—in a helpless position waiting and praying for assistance. Then imagine how you would feel if you knew that your fleet could not get to you in time—but that they would not ask for help from someone who possibly could. That is the legacy of pride, and how our pride hurts others.

Another Boat in Distress

The Gospel of Matthew (Chapter 8) records the story of a boat in distress, though in this story the difficulties came through no one's fault. There was no negligence, poor judgment or faulty equipment; when at sea, sometimes storms just happen. The terrified crew eventually cried for help—which came in an unexpected way. This is how it occurred and, more importantly, how it ended.

Following the instructions of Jesus, the disciples entered a boat to cross to the opposite shore of the Sea of Galilee. Jesus, weary from the day's events, was sleeping soundly in the stern of the boat, resting on a cushion. As the disciples began rowing that dark evening, it's likely the sea was calm. They were temporarily away from the crushing crowds that thronged Jesus everywhere. It was blissfully quiet—even peaceful—as a night at sea can be.

But storms can strike quickly on the Sea of Galilee without warning. The pear-shaped lake, roughly 13 by 7.5 miles at its widest points, is ringed by mountainous terrain. While the Sea of Galilee is 680 feet below sea level, the hills to the east side of the lake reach over 2,000 feet. This creates temperature differences where cool, dry air from the hills funnels through the mounds, rushing suddenly onto the lake's surface. A calm sea quickly can turn violent, as it did on this evening.

The boat was gliding through the inky sea when suddenly fierce winds arose; the unforeseeable storm these fishermen feared struck with fury. Driving and pounding rain began filling the boat, which rode lower and lower in the water. Doubtless, the disciples baled furiously with cupped hands or anything they could find, but to no avail; the water line inside the boat crept up inch by dreadful inch. At the rate the boat was filling there seemed no other possible outcome. The boat would be swamped, and all aboard likely drowned. The disciples were experienced sailors, not novices given to overreaction, and their terror was genuine.

Remarkably, as the boat filled and the winds lashed their faces, Jesus remained fast asleep at his spot in the back of the boat. Was he drenched from the rain? Was part of his body submerged in the pooling water? Regardless of all around him, he slept, fully at peace. The disciples may have wondered: how is he sleeping through this? Surely he'll wake any minute now. Perhaps they did not even think about him at all until the last moment. Finally, the distraught disciples could stand it no longer. They roused him roughly, their terrified voices asking: *don't you care that we are dying?*

It was the same question put to the Prophet Jonah as he slept through a squall that terrified experienced sailors. *Don't you care that we are dying?* (We will see Jonah's story in a later chapter). The disciples were convinced that their end was near. Had Jesus not been in the boat it was likely the case. There was a pressing need, and the solution seemed logical. Once roused, Jesus stood and commanded the storm to cease; the command was literally: "Be muzzled." Immediately the storm ceased, exactly as ordered, to the amazement of the disciples. "Who is this," they wondered "that even commands a storm to cease and it obeys?" *(Matthew 8:23-27)*

Seeking Help

There is nothing particularly noble or heroic about calling for help when you are in need; it is an instinctive and often wise reaction. When someone does not call because of a competing motivation—like pride—we generally see it as a foolish choice. Of course, the decision of the men in the Kremlin about the *Kursk* was made easier since they themselves were not *in* the sub. Had they been present with radio contact to the surface, their reactions might have been very different.

Nonetheless, the knowledge of one's limitations and willingness to seek help are marks of maturity and even wisdom. It's quite another issue for us when those who are able to help refuse to do so. Part of being in a boat of distress is inevitably a sense of helplessness and dependency.

Now, here is the odd part of the story of the sudden storm on the Sea of Galilee. The disciples, experienced fishermen, knew they were in serious trouble. In fact, based on how things were going they assumed they would not survive the ordeal—and were likely correct *under ordinary circumstances.* And so, they woke the sleeping Savior with the panicked urgency that facing death brings. The really curious part of the story comes after Jesus rebuked the storm and it ceased. As the startled disciples were watching the storm die down, Jesus turned to them and asked: *Why are you so fearful? How is it that you had no faith? (Matthew 8:26)* It is positively a rebuke—a charge they were fearful and faithless. Weren't the disciples making a reasonable request? Isn't knowing your limitations and asking for help the reasonable thing to do? Evidently it was not in this case.

It is far too easy to draw the obvious conclusion; the disciples should have had faith and trusted in Jesus. I am sure of one thing in reading this account. If I had been there, I would have wakened Jesus well before they did. Why was it a lack of faith to call for help in that perilous situation? It was because help was already there; the disciples just did not recognize it.

Believers in Christ who find themselves in a boat called distress will likely call on God by habit or conditioning; they might even do so with urgency or desperation. It may be as a last resort after we have tried "every other option"—the equivalent of a football "Hail Mary pass." Yet, this is not necessarily a bad thing. Despite the rebuke to the disciples, I do not think the call for help itself was the issue in that sinking boat. In fact, the Bible is filled with references encouraging people to call on God in their distress. There seems to be another factor at work here, and it may be this: once we have the assurance that Jesus is with us in our boat of distress everything changes. The frantic call to God asks for assurance and help; once God "shows up" at the scene, the answer—or the assurance—is in place. The storm may continue to rage; the wind of affliction may lash at our face while the rain of circumstances pelts our body and fills the boat steadily. It may seem that our God and Savior is sleeping on the job, but He is not—*and accepting that is an act of faith.*

Before the disciples entered the boat, Mark's Gospel (telling the same story) records Jesus saying: *"Let us cross over to the other side." (Mark 4:35)* Once the God of the universe gave this instruction, there was no place on earth or sea safer. No ocean liner could have been more secure on the little lake that evening. The essence of faith was that nothing could happen while God was present except for what He allowed. The lack of faith was not a simple case of calling for help; rather, it was fear and doubt while obeying a direct instruction from the God of the universe, and in his very presence.

How does this fit in with the tragedy of the *Kursk?* A boat in distress, like the stricken sub, needed help and needed it quickly. Pride delayed the call, and possibly doomed the surviving crew. In the distress of our lives, pride will separate us from God and lead us to foolish and even tragic choices. But calling for help is only part of the story. The greatest source of help in our distress is a loving and merciful God. *A cry for help is a good beginning but a poor ending if it never roots in faith.* In the end, a pitiful cry that will not trust God is simply another form of pride. It is the other side of the coin that elevates and follows self instead of God. Do not be confused by *manifestations* of pride; whether we roar or whimper is not the issue: it is whether we trust God in our circumstances.

Getting Out of a Boat Called Distress

It is the common destiny of humanity to know distress. We all live with the reality that death is inevitable in this world, at least until the time our Savior comes to fulfill his promise to make all things new. When Jesus taught His disciples about the tribulations of life, He did not speak of them as *possibilities.* We are all, so to speak, building a house, which is the edifice of our life.

The events and choices of our lives fit together, brick by brick, to make the dwelling of our destiny. Each house is destined to experience the storms of life; Jesus described it this way:

> *Therefore whoever hears these sayings of Mine, and does them, I will liken to a wise man who built his house on a rock: and the rain fell and floods came, and the winds blew and beat against that house; and it did not fall, for it was built on the rock. But everyone who hears these sayings of Mine and does not obey them, will be like a fool who built his house on the sand: and the rain fell and floods came, and the winds blew and beat against that house; and it fell. And great was its fall.* (Mt 7: 24-27)

Notice that Jesus did not teach *"if* winds should blow..."The scene he described is inevitable in every life: just as it happened with the disciples in the boat, the winds and torrential rain *will* come. Both houses in the parable are built the same way, and face the same trials; the only difference is the *foundation.*

Foundations are the assumptions—the "givens" if you prefer—upon which all else rests. They are the lenses through which we view everything and interpret all events. Two people will experience the same event with completely different responses because of the foundational assumptions in their lives.

How did the disciples finally exit a boat called distress? It was by the saving work of their Lord who intended they go to the opposite shore. There was nothing they could do in their own power to get out of that boat. There were no rescue ships, no technology, and swimming to shore was a very poor option. We get out of a boat of distress by trusting fully in a loving Savior, and the faith that nothing can happen to us without His awareness. To use another of the Lord's parables about storms, it is a matter of having the right foundation in our lives. If the foundation is built on Christ, the house will stand, no matter how severe the tempest.

The way out of a boat of distress is not through *outward* action, but through the inward process of *faith*. It is not accomplished with activity, but rather stillness rooted in trust. It is not aided by frantic calls for help, but finds its truth in the inner peace that passes understanding. It does not focus on circumstances with dread, but believes that God's wisdom allows all for His purposes. It is the extraordinary faith described in the Book of Romans that declares: "*For all things work together for good for those who love God, and are the called according to His purposes.*" (Rom. 8:28) In a paradoxical twist, we get out of the boat by staying in the boat, but seeing through the situation through the eyes of Christ.

It is the faith that sustains us with the belief that God loves us profoundly and more deeply than the mind can comprehend. *This* is the way out of the boat called distress. We may step out of the boat on the shore of this life, or we may leave it on the shore of a far more beautiful and distant land that God has prepared in eternity for those who love Him. If He is with us on the boat, we will certainly step out on the shore He desires. Our part is to believe and not doubt in His seeming silence.

Solomon Ginsburg

Solomon Ginsburg was born in Poland in 1867, the son of Jewish parents. His father was a rabbi, and young Solomon seemed destined to follow in his footsteps. To his father's horror, while living in London, Solomon heard the gospel from a Jewish believer in Jesus as the Messiah and converted to Christianity. His conversion would bring intense persecution. On one occasion, he was savagely beaten and left for dead in a garbage box with multiple broken bones, soaked in blood and unconscious. He later referred to this and other persecutions as "glorious times."

Solomon would go on to experience a powerful ministry in Brazil, where he labored for 35 years as a missionary. He would later be called "The Apostle of Brazil" by many people, a fit name considering the churches in Brazil under his ministry increased from two in 1891 to 820 seven years before his death in 1927. He would write about his adventures and struggles in his autobiography, "A Wandering Jew in Brazil."

A lesser known story about Solomon took place in 1911. After an exhausting series of evangelical meetings in Europe, Solomon decided to take a furlough and visit America. His plans took him through Lisbon, where he planned to travel to London and then on to America. While in Lisbon, he heard reports of fierce storms raging in the Bay of Biscay, through which he would travel to reach London. It would be a dangerous trip, and he was advised to wait a week and catch a different ship to London. He was fearful of the news, but while praying about what he should do, read Deuteronomy 2:7 in his devotional reading: *For the Lord your God has blessed you in all the work of your hand. He knows your trudging through this great wilderness. These forty years the Lord your God has been with you; you have lacked nothing.*

Solomon felt that the Lord had spoken to him through this verse, and that God's protection had been upon him in all his many travels. If God was with him, he did not need to fear weather reports. And so, with no further trepidation he boarded the boat in Lisbon and arrived in London without incident.

In London, he caught the *Majestic* and enjoyed a peaceful and uneventful trans-Atlantic voyage. After landing in New York, Solomon made a startling discovery. If he had waited a week, as he was advised, he would have missed his berth on the *Majestic* and taken the next ship leaving London. That ship would have been the *Titanic*.[4]

CHAPTER TWO: A BOAT CALLED DISBELIEF

"We are all in the same boat in a stormy sea, and we owe each other a terrible loyalty."
G.K. Chesterton

The Lusitania

Crowds bustled excitedly around New York's Pier 54 on the fateful morning of May 1, 1915. Many were there to board the most famous ocean liner in the world, the *Lusitania*. First launched in 1906, *Lusitania* was a technical and engineering marvel. She was the first liner to cross the Atlantic in under five days, the pride of the British owned Cunard line. On that May morning, *Lusitania* was filled with nearly 2,000 occupants, including many American families with children. The mood was festive as the massive liner churned and crept from its mooring, well-wishers and the curious waving to those on board. The ship was traveling to England, and with good conditions would be there in a week or less.

But as the *Lusitania* sat in port, passengers and crew eager to start the voyage, there was an ominous undertone. The newspapers in New York that very day ran an ad from the German government, placed in some instances next to the *Lusitania's* own advertisement.

The world knew too well that a state of war existed between Germany and its allies, and England and France and their allies. Although officially neutral, it was generally known that the United States was selling arms to England. This, coupled with the boat's destination, made for a tense atmosphere. The warning, reproduced below, read as follows:

NOTICE!

TRAVELLERS intending to embark on the Atlantic voyage are reminded that a state of war exists between Germany and her allies and Great Britain and her allies; that the zone of war includes the waters adjacent to the British Isles; that, in accordance with formal notice given by the Imperial German Government, vessels flying the flag of Great Britain, or any of her allies, are liable to destruction in those waters and that travellers sailing in the war zone on the ships of Great Britain or her allies do so at their own risk.

IMPERIAL GERMAN EMBASSY,
Washington, D.C. 22nd April 1915

Many among the passengers were disturbed by the warning, ominously placed next to advertisements for *Lusitania's* return voyage. The *Lusitania's* captain, William Thomas Turner, did his best to assure the passengers—and crew—that the ship was not in danger. Even if the Germans intended to attack a passenger ship, a doubtful proposition with Americans aboard, the *Lusitania's* speed made it very difficult for submarines to catch, let alone accurately fire torpedoes. The submarine technology of that day was primitive, even by WWII standards, and so Turner and others were confident the *Lusitania* would be safe, even if it drew hostile fire. Though the ship's speed was certainly an asset, the captain and crew should have been on high alert. All knew that a number of British merchant ships had already been sunk by German submarines. In retrospect, *Lusitania's* owners did not believe the Germans would sink a civilian liner, particularly one coming from (at that time) a neutral America with a large number of American citizens.

The Sinking of the Lusitania

Lusitania steamed out of New York at noon on May 1st, two hours behind schedule. Even as it traversed the North Atlantic, the German Submarine *U-20* was busy at the business of war. Lurking in waters off the coast of Ireland between May 5th and 6th, the U-20 sank three British vessels. The Royal Navy reportedly sent warnings to all British vessels near or approaching the area, the message getting to Captain Turner on the evening of February 6th. At about 11:00 AM on May 7th, Captain Turner received another warning, and taking evasive measures, changed his course to take the ship nearer to land where he assumed it would be safer.

Lusitania was still about 30 miles out from Cape Clear Island on the southern tip of Ireland when she ran into a heavy fog. She reduced her speed to 18 knots, or about 20 MPH, on a course that would take her right into the path of the U-20. The reduction in speed made her a more inviting target for the submarine, which according to some accounts was down to its last few torpedoes and low on fuel.

On other occasions, German submarines gave warnings before sinking a ship—even letting passengers enter lifeboats first in a few instances. The *U-20*, however, would not have dared to send a warning to the *Lusitania*. With its enormous size and potential for speed, ramming the sub as a defensive measure was a perilous but feasible alternative for the liner. On the afternoon of May 7th at about 3:00 PM, the submarine suddenly sighted the Lusitania, not more than 800 meters away. The captain of the submarine immediately ordered all hands to battle stations and prepared a torpedo for firing.

There is an unsubstantiated story that after the order to fire was given, a crewmember on the *U-20* named Charles Voegele refused to obey, being unwilling to take the lives of innocent women and children. The account of Voegele's refusal also says he was later court-martialed for insubordination. Whether true or not, the torpedo was fired and struck the *Lusitania* on the starboard side just below the bridge. As the torpedo hit, a ghastly cloud of debris spiraled skyward, crippling the ship. Captain Schweiger of the *U-20* would describe the hit this way in the sub's log:

> *Torpedo hits starboard side right behind the bridge. An unusually heavy explosion takes place with a very strong explosive cloud. The explosion of the torpedo must have been followed by a second one [boiler or coal or powder?]... The ship stops immediately and heels over to starboard very quickly, immersing simultaneously at the bow... the name Lusitania becomes visible in golden letters.*

The *U-20* log verified the sub fired only one torpedo, though there is some controversy over this claim because a second blast rocked the *Lusitania* within minutes of the strike. Some believe it was a second torpedo, while others maintain it was an explosion of coal dust, or even ammunition (which the boat was carrying). Most likely we will never know the source of the second explosion, but that next blast caused the ship to sink rapidly. Panic ensued immediately throughout the stricken vessel, and Captain Turner gave an abrupt order to abandon ship. Worse yet, the ship would not respond to efforts to steer or reduce speed. It would be a full ten minutes until the flooding in the hold would slow the ship enough to safely launch the lifeboats.

Following the tragedy of the *Titanic* only three years earlier, the *Lusitania* had been fitted with enough lifeboats for everyone aboard. Even with this precaution, the severe listing of the ship, and initially the speed, prevented the boats from launching safely. More significantly, the crippled ship sank in just eighteen minutes. During this brief interval the ship erupted into pandemonium as lifeboats slammed into the sea, overturning and spilling passengers into the water. By some disputed accounts, passengers were crushed by lifeboats that crashed onto and slid down the deck. Other boats in the water tipped as panicked passengers leaped and clawed to get in. Of the 48 lifeboats on the ship, enough for every passenger and crew member, only 6 launched successfully. Other passengers managed to cling to debris from the ship, including collapsible lifeboats that washed off the deck.

Captain Turner remained in the bridge doing all he could until water smashed through the cabin doors and flooded the bridge, sweeping him into the ocean. Turner managed to find a chair floating in the ocean, and kept afloat while the ship went down. He was pulled into a rescue boat three hours later, unconscious, but survived, and later provided information on *Lusitania's* course that allowed the remains of the ship to be found. During the ensuing chaos, the captain of the *U-20* watched through his periscope; as the great stricken liner lurched under the surface, he calmly retracted the periscope and put out to sea.

Lusitania's bow slammed into the surface of the ocean floor 330 feet below the surface, almost two miles from the spot where she was torpedoed. As she sank, the ship's boilers exploded, tearing the ship into fragments. After her bow went down, the stern lurched briefly above the water and then sank below, leaving only scattered pieces of debris and bodies strewn about the scene. Of the 1,959 people on board, 1,198 perished that day, including almost 100 children. Fewer than 300 bodies were recovered from the sea, with most of the victims entombed within the ship.

The Aftermath

Reaction was swift and strong on both sides of the Atlantic, with the US Government condemning the attack. Americans were outraged to learn that 128 US citizens were among the dead. The day following the attack, the former German Colonial Secretary made a statement in Cleveland, Ohio. The statement was the first in a series of responses from the Imperial German Government claiming the *Lusitania* was carrying "contraband of war." The German Government believed that fair warning had been given, and the ship was a legitimate target once it entered a war zone. The Collector of the Port of New York, who had inspected the cargo before departure, issued a strong denial, saying the ship had no arms or ammunition, and would not have been permitted to load such weapons while docked in New York. A N.Y. Times article days later acknowledged that the ship did indeed have 4,200 cases of cartridges for small arms, though it disputed that these qualified as ammunition for a war effort. In 2008, divers exploring the wreck found about four million rounds of U.S. manufactured ammunition, which confirmed the long-held suspicion that the *Lusitania* was carrying supplies for the war effort.

Despite official German accounts defending the sub's actions, German citizens were angry with their government for both the attack and the attempts to justify it. Even Germany's allies, Austria, Hungary and Turkey, criticized the attack. To placate the Americans and keep the U.S. neutral in the war, Germany gave an assurance to President Woodrow Wilson that there would be no further attacks under their "sink on sight" policy. Nonetheless, the incident caused tensions between America and Germany, and started swaying American public opinion that formerly opposed entering the war. Following Germany's resumption of unrestricted submarine warfare in 1917, the U.S. officially entered WWI.

Looking back on the incident of the *Lusitania,* one sees conflicting assumptions and beliefs on both sides of the tragedy. It's likely the Cunard Line did not believe a U-Boat would attack a liner with civilian passengers departing from a neutral nation. Captain Turner probably shared this belief, though he also trusted his ship's speed as a back-up emergency measure. The Germans did not believe the claim that the ship had no weapons or ammunition for the war effort. While merchant ships were fair game and subject to attack under the then recognized "rules" of war, carrying munitions in a passenger vessel was a dangerous shell game. The Germans also likely thought placing the newspaper ad would discourage American citizens from sailing on the ship, as well as giving cover for their actions.

Beliefs and perceptions determine our actions in every area of life, including the spiritual realm. In the tragic case of the *Lusitania*, disbelief on both sides led to a high stakes game in which a called bluff proved fatal for almost 1,200 souls.

A Boat In A Storm

Visitors looking at the Sea of Galilee for the first time often have an emotional reaction. It was, after all, the center of so much of Jesus' earthly ministry. The serenity conceals the ferocity and chaos of storms that strike suddenly. One example is found in the story where Jesus slept in the back of a boat while the quaking disciples feared for their lives. A story of a different storm ends with another astonishing demonstration that Jesus is Lord of the elements, and all creation.

Matthew tells the story this way:

> *Immediately Jesus made the disciples get into the boat and go on ahead of him to the other side, while he dismissed the crowd. After he had dismissed them, he went up on a mountainside by himself to pray. When evening came, he was there alone, but the boat was already a considerable distance from land, buffeted by the waves because the wind was against it. During the fourth watch of the night Jesus went out to them, walking on the lake. When the disciples saw him walking on the lake, they were terrified. "It's a ghost," they said, and cried out in fear.*
>
> *But Jesus immediately said to them: "Take courage! It is I. Don't be afraid."*
>
> *"Lord, if it's you," Peter replied, "tell me to come to you on the water."*
>
> *"Come," he said. Then Peter got down out of the boat, walked on the water and came toward Jesus. But when he saw the wind, he was afraid and, beginning to sink, cried out, "Lord, save me!" Immediately Jesus reached out his hand and caught him. "You of little faith," he said, "why did you doubt?" And when they climbed into the boat, the wind died down. Then those who were in the boat worshiped him, saying, "Truly you are the Son of God."*
> (Matthew 14: 22-33, NIV)

The first thing to note is that Jesus "made" them go; the sense of the original Greek is that He *compelled* them. Mark's parallel account adds these details:

> *When evening came, the boat was in the middle of the lake, and he was alone on land. He saw the disciples straining at the oars, because the wind was against them. About the fourth watch of the night he went out to them, walking on the lake. He was about to pass by them, but when they saw him walking on the lake, they thought he was a ghost. They cried out, because they*

all saw him and were terrified. Immediately he spoke to them and said, "Take courage! It is I. Don't be afraid." Then he climbed into the boat with them, and the wind died down. They were completely amazed, for they had not understood about the loaves; their hearts were hardened. (Mark 6: 47-52 NIV)

To set the story, it is the "fourth watch," or between 3:00—6:00 AM. The disciples strained at their oars as the wind whipped against them, making movement slow and labored. They were certainly on their guard, knowing that strong winds could turn into chaotic storms quickly. The fishermen of those days avoided sailing too far from shore for fear of storms—just like this one. But the disciples persevered here; the Lord had ordered them to travel to the opposite shore, and so they labored away.

Jesus watched as they struggled, their progress excruciatingly slow, rough hands and heavy hearts wearied by the force of nature's whim. Were they in danger? Had they reached the limits of their endurance? Jesus decided to go to them. He may have pulled the cord that hoisted His garment, freeing his legs for easier movement, and strode to the water's edge. Then, one leg thrust out onto the water, sandal firmly planted, followed by the other foot, walking toward the struggling disciples on a raging sea. He kept them in view, though in an odd twist, walked close to the boat and made as if He would walk right past them. Every new detail brings two questions to mind. Why was Jesus walking past them? He surely knew they would see Him, and knew what their reaction would be. Was walking by them designed to get this reaction? Or teach them something? Meditating on these questions plumbs the mind of God; it's not possible to do anything but guess.

What we do know is how the disciples reacted. As the figure approached, indistinct in the gloomy and stormy horizon, the astonished disciples shrieked in pure terror. It must be a ghost, maybe risen from the abyss of the sea. Mark's gospel says their amazed terror came from their "hardened hearts." The Greek for heart, *kardia*, refers to the heart of what makes a person: the psychological core or conscious awareness and spiritual responsiveness of an individual. [1] In other words, the fear came from an unbelieving and unperceiving heart; in short, a heart of disbelief.

Getting Out of a Boat of Disbelief

Jesus let the disciples struggle, but only to a point—in order to make a point. He must have been fairly close to the boat; close enough to be heard over the wind, though just far enough to be hazy. His voice rang out emphatically: "take courage! It is I." There was no need to fear; the "ghost" was Jesus Himself, and He had come to them. And then a second time: "Do not be afraid." Then, in an act of incredible courage, the impulsive Peter called back: *If it is you, ask me to come out to you.* Jesus' response was a single word, though no word could have been weightier in that storm-tossed sea: "Come." Then Peter made the decision to get out of a boat called Disbelief.

How do you imagine Peter left that boat? Did he leap over casually—like you might hop over a low fence? Here's how I picture it: Astonished faces around the boat, mouths agape, stared at Peter. Conflicting thoughts whirled through their minds: Is he really going to do it? Will we have to rescue him? Is it really Jesus out there off the side of the boat? Is Peter crazy? As if in response, Peter's face hardened with determination. His sturdy hands gripped the side of the boat, and he slowly raised one muscular leg up and over the side. He let his foot rest on top of the water and pressed down a little: it felt firm. Then, slowly straightening, he increased the pressure and swung his other leg over. Relieved, he felt it firm to both feet. Then, with an enormous effort of focused will, he righted himself, released his hands, and stood next to the boat. His mind reeled processing his actions. *He was standing on top of the sea!* And then, eyes straight ahead on the still indistinct figure, he placed one foot forward—and walked.

The rest of the story is well known. Peter's focus, literally and spiritually, shifted from Jesus to the circumstances, in this case the wind. Sudden doubt flickered in his mind; this was impossible! Look at these waves and wind: this can't be happening! And so he began to sink, crying out as his body submerged. Then Jesus' strong grip clasped his hand and forearm, drawing him back to the surface. Firm but tender eyes met his as the Master asked: *Why did you lose faith? Why did you doubt?*

Before glibly rushing in to comment on this wondrous story, a few preliminaries are in order. First, any one of us on that boat would have been just as terrified by the sight of someone walking on water towards the boat. I'd have likely yelled louder than anyone there that night. Second, I doubt that it would have occurred to one in a hundred to think of leaving the boat to prove it was Jesus, and even after the call, I am skeptical that one in a thousand would have done what Peter did. Whatever may be said about a lack of faith, I have never met—or even heard of—someone walking on water that was not frozen. Any comments on what Peter did must, with respect and trembling, recognize how much more poorly we would have fared.

While much could be said (and has been) about this story, I would like to focus a few modest thoughts on one small sliver of the account. Looking at Peter's example, *how do we get out of a boat of Disbelief?* Disbelief in this case was rooted in fear of circumstances. Common sense would tell us not to leave this boat, and the circumstances spell danger. What are the lessons for us from Peter's extraordinary act of faith and courage?

First, accept fear as part of the cost of spiritual growth. What we trust, by the very nature of that act, becomes familiar and therefore comfortable; leaving that comfort zone brings fear, which is a prerequisite for spiritual growth. We can be certain that Peter experienced healthy fear before taking his first step. As is often said, courage is not the absence of fear, but the willingness to go forward when we are afraid.

Second, we leave a boat of Disbelief *at the call of Jesus*. Peter did not step out of the boat until Jesus said *"Come."* The scriptures repeatedly commend *faith*, but not *presumption*. The Bible affirms that without faith it is impossible to please God. Yet, faith disconnected from God's word easily drifts into presumption. Jesus Himself was once tempted this way by Satan, and urged to leap from the pinnacle of the great Temple in Jerusalem. The challenge was put to Jesus as an act of faith, though it clearly was not God's will. Satan's suggestion to jump quoted scripture saying that God would protect His Son and that Jesus would suffer no harm. Jesus' rebuke of Satan went right to the heart of true faith versus presumption: *"It is written you shall not tempt the Lord your God."* (Luke 4: 9-12) Faith is obeying the call of Jesus, the Word of God—not indulging in our own agenda. But part of faith is also waiting until we hear the call of God. Faith is often a call to patience as well as action.

Third, we leave the boat knowing that *God's call is His enabling*. Like Peter, it may be a slow and tentative exit. We may test the water, so to speak, because of circumstances. But the call of God means He has enabled us to do what He has asked. We do not have to worry about our lack of qualifications, stature, resources or natural abilities. The natural excuses of life simply don't apply when the call of God comes. In fact, the scripture assures us He uses the foolish things of the world to confound the wise. (1 Cor. 1:27) Rather than worry about what we *think* we are able to accomplish, the real question is *has God called me to take this step?* This should be the focus of our prayers, counsel with others, and seeking the will of God in our lives. It cannot be said often enough: when He calls us to leave the boat of Disbelief, he will enable according to His call.

Fourth, we should leave a boat of Disbelief with our eyes fixed on Jesus and not the circumstances. Peter did not begin to sink until he removed his eyes from Jesus and placed them on the wind and waves. Focusing on the circumstances in the storms of life brings fear—or a lack of faith. Importantly, faith is grounded in the knowledge of who Jesus is and His love for us, and not whether circumstances line up with our wishes. Faith does not seek to control, but rather to trust and obey. Making Jesus our focus in the worst storms of life is not easy. We naturally want to focus on circumstances more than God. The storm has visible and threatening manifestations, while the unseen God ministers in a quiet and stilled heart. The decision to trust God in our trials requires that we make Him our focus; turning our eyes to the circumstances causes us to sink.

Fifth, and finally, we leave this boat knowing that failure is part of the process. Peter took a few steps before fear and doubt gripped him. Failure is a learning process and not a blot on our character. Remember the attitude of Thomas Edison, who said: *"Results? Why, man, I have gotten lots of results! If I find 10,000 ways something won't work, I haven't failed. I am not discouraged, because every wrong attempt discarded is often a step forward…"* Even though Peter floundered and started sinking, here is the remarkable part of the story: Peter walked on water. With focused faith, we can climb out of a boat called Disbelief and do extraordinary things for God.

C.S. Lewis

C.S. Lewis is undoubtedly one of the best known and beloved names in the history of the Christian faith. The Cambridge and Oxford don was a brilliant professor of medieval literature, but also wrote fiction, poetry, allegorical tales and memorable books in defense of the faith. His Chronicles of Narnia still captivate children and adults alike, and classics like Mere Christianity and The Screwtape Letters are reprinted every year and discovered by new generations.

Popular images of Lewis abound, usually strolling the English countryside in professorial Tweeds, or sitting in his study puffing his meerschaum pipe. His life, however, was not always the idyllic and detached life of an academic. His childhood was emotionally fragile after the death of his mother, and he suffered under arbitrary and even brutal schoolmasters. By his own account, he was lonely, unathletic and tended toward introspection. His academic career was cut short by conscription in WWI, where he witnessed the horrors of trench warfare. Lewis would suffer wounds from an exploding shell before finally returning to Oxford and his beloved teaching duties. Of all the struggles in Lewis' life, though, perhaps the least known and understood were his battles with disbelief. He would start life as an atheist before his celebrated conversion to Christ, but would wrestle again with faith in his latter years during the most painful trial of his adult life.

Lewis' journey to faith is recounted in his autobiography, *Surprised By Joy.* For a young man so steeped in atheism and what he called "rationalism," he would later declare: "Looking back on my life now, I am astonished that I did not progress into the opposite orthodoxy—did not become a Leftist, Atheist, satiric Intellectual of the type we all know so well."

Of the process that led to his faith in Christ, Lewis would later say: "*Really, a young atheist cannot guard his faith too carefully. Dangers lie in wait for him on every side… All my acts, desires, and thoughts were to be brought into harmony with universal Spirit. For the first time I examined myself with a seriously practical purpose. And there I found what appalled me; a zoo of lusts, a bedlam of ambitions, a nursery of fears, a harem of fondled hatreds. My name was Legion.*" [2] One such "danger" was an acquaintance that Lewis called "the hardest boiled of all the atheists I ever knew." When that man casually remarked that the evidence for the historical gospel was surprisingly good, Lewis felt as if there was no safe place of escape. Finally, alone in his room, the "most dejected and reluctant convert in all England" dropped to his knees and prayed, a prodigal coming to his Father. Unlike the prodigal, who returned home willingly, Lewis described his coming to God "kicking, struggling (and) resentful," and even more astonishingly, encountering a loving God who welcomed him on those terms.

The Death of Joy

From his reluctant conversion, Lewis blazed into prominence in England. During WWII, his broadcast talks on the Christian faith on BBC radio were so popular that they were later incorporated into his perennial best seller *Mere Christianity*. Though growing in reputation, Lewis kept to the life of a bachelor and cloistered academic. By his own admission, life as a single man was "safe" from emotional demands and intimacy. Lewis' carefully constructed safety, however, would come crashing to an end when he became friendly with a divorced woman named Joy Davidman.

Lewis and Joy, then Joy Gresham, met in 1952. The 54 year old Lewis and his brother agreed to meet Gresham for tea on her visit to London to find a publisher. Gresham was an award winning poet, married at the time to acclaimed author Bill Gresham. The marriage was already unhappy, and Joy finally left her husband after he announced he had taken up with another woman. Lewis was taken with Joy from their first meeting, Her lively intellect and vibrant Christian faith made her welcome in his life; better yet, she would never back down from a battle of wits.

Years after their first meeting, Joy returned to take up residence in London with her two sons. When her visa was in jeopardy, she asked Lewis (who was by this time a friend) to marry her in name only so she could remain in the country as his spouse. He agreed, though their relationship was strictly platonic. They quietly and privately entered into a civil marriage, though they continued living separate lives apart. Although Lewis may not have intended it or even seen it coming, the spiritual and emotional bonds between them continued to grow. Eventually, on what all believed to be Gresham's death bed from a running battle with cancer, Lewis proposed a "true" marriage. Gresham happily accepted, and this time the couple had a Christian marriage ceremony.

Then, miraculously, Joy's cancer went into remission. The marriage rapidly blossomed with a genuine honeymoon, followed by a whirlwind of passion. A lifetime of restrained intimate emotions gushed in torrents from Lewis during their few married years. And then, with hideous swiftness, the cancer returned with a vengeance. Lewis would watch his beloved wife die in great suffering, though she told a priest on her deathbed that she had made her peace with God. He remained by her bedside, begging her through tears not to leave him, until she succumbed to her illness.

Following her death in 1960, about three years before Lewis' own death, the great author and Christian thinker who had inspired millions of people was a shattered man. He recorded his pain over a few months in a series of notebooks that would later be published as *A Grief Observed*. Here, he realized, was the great paradox of love. He had led his life "safe" from emotional attachments, but the nut finally had been cracked late in life. He had finally risked emotional vulnerability and savored the fullness of love, only to have it quickly ripped away, leaving the deepest sort of pain. His decades of theoretical thinking on suffering suddenly rang hollow. He began to wonder whether God might be a cosmic sadist or worse.

Lewis would write "Meanwhile, where is God...? (G)o to him when your need is desperate, when all other help is vain, and what do you find? A door slammed in your face, and a sound of bolting and double-bolting on the inside. After that, silence. You may as well turn away." He would turn the lens on his personal agony as well: "The most precious gift that marriage gave me was this constant impact of something very close and intimate yet all the time unmistakably other, resistant—in a word, real. Is all that work to be undone...? *Oh God, God, why did you take such trouble to force this creature out of its shell if it is now doomed to crawl back—to be sucked back—into it?*"

The Victory Over Disbelief

Lewis would gradually hear the beckoning call of the God in whom he had put his trust. His deepest pain, inexplicable to him, became an invitation to trust God and resume the course. He began to think of God as the path to be reunited with Joy; if there was truly a Heaven, would he not see her there? Might things again become as they once were here—in the happiest time of his life? And then the thought struck him that God must not be a *path*, but an end in Himself.:

> *"But then of course I know perfectly well that He can't be used as a road. If you're approaching Him not as a goal but as the road, not as the end but as a means, you're not really approaching Him at all... Lord, are these your real terms? Can I meet (Joy) again only if I learn to love you so much that I don't care whether I meet her or not?"*

The conclusion of *A Grief Observed* is a quiet but profound triumph for Lewis. He finally comes to see—or more importantly *experience*—the love of God in his tragedy. *"For this is one of the miracles of love; it gives—to both, but perhaps especially to the woman—a power of seeing through its own enchantments and yet not being disenchanted. To see, in some measure, like God. His love and His knowledge are not distinct from one another, nor from Him. We could almost say He sees because He loves, and therefore loves although He sees."*

Like the Apostle Peter so many centuries before him, Lewis was able to see an indistinct presence of God and hear His call, beckoning him from his boat. Regardless of the circumstances and feelings, there could be only one truth. Either God was real and understood his pain, or He was not. For Lewis, there was only one possible answer: where else can I go when you alone have the words of eternal life?

The very nature of intimate love risks loss and pain. Although Lewis had experienced death in many forms, he had never been touched by death in intimacy. Interestingly, the piles of mangled and frozen corpses in the horrors of trench warfare did not keep him from finding faith in Christ—nor did the death of family members or professional acquaintances. It took the risk of intimacy to coax him from his safe harbor into the storm that pierced his soul; in his most painful moments he would question everything he believed. And, as so many before him, Lewis found that when all is stripped away and no sense or logic will adequately explain, there is a peace of God that passes understanding.

CHAPTER THREE: A BOAT CALLED DISOBEDIENCE

"Does any one know where the love of God goes when the waves turn the minutes to hours?"
The Wreck of the Edmund Fitzgerald

"And the sea gave up the dead who were in it..."
Revelation 20:13

The Andrea Gail

Nearly all cultures abound with stories and legends about boats. From the ill-fated voyages of Odysseus, to the powerful imagery of *Moby Dick,* boats have fascinated and captivated our imaginations. One modern true story made into a popular movie was the tale of the ill-fated *Andrea Gail,* told in the movie *The Perfect Storm.*

The story has so worked its way into our own culture that the expression *a perfect storm* is a popular metaphor for multiple events going awry, and in combination producing disastrous consequences. One can only imagine the feeling of helplessness of a crew, trapped in a small cabin, while their boat sits atop a monstrous wave. The sea ahead drops down into a valley, and the boat races headlong like a small plaything. With this comes the realization—the sickening certainty—that death is near.

Captain Billy Tyne was an experienced and reliable skipper, and the pilot of the 72 foot *Andrea Gail*. His boat was a "longliner,"a name for swordfish boats that lay miles of line in their fishing routine. He and his crew of five were counting on a good run when they steamed out of Gloucester harbor in late September, 1991. On this last trip of the season, Billy and crew were hoping to catch over 40,000 pounds of swordfish. The crew worked on a risky arrangement; after covering expenses and the owner's cut, they would split the profits. A bountiful catch meant high profits, but a poor catch could be ruinous.

Swordfish excursions are arduous and dangerous trips. A usual run is about a month, away from loved ones and places to spend the money a crew hopes to earn. Working 20 hour days is common, and the tedium and strain of one day flows seamlessly into another. The combination of dangerous heavy equipment, the elements and fatigue makes commercial fishing the most lethal profession in the world, with more deaths per capita than police, firefighters, or emergency rescue squads. Sebastian Junger's account of "The Perfect Storm" notes that since 1650, it is estimated that ten thousand fishermen have died from the Town of Gloucester alone. The threat of death or horrific injury is a constant companion in commercial fishing.

Why do crews willingly suffer the dangers and strains of this life? One big reason is the money. A fishing trip is a form of gambling, and everyone wants to hit the jackpot. It's very difficult for unskilled workers, in other legal jobs, to make what a good run brings in. The risk is shared by the friends and families of the crews. Traditional homes in New England were built with a "Widow's Walk." This was a simple platform with a view of the sea, where the spouses of mariners gazed at the ocean, desperately hoping, praying, and mostly waiting for the sight of returning ships. Even today, one hears stories of floors worn out from constant, anxious pacing.

The poignancy of imminent death at sea was captured by Sebastian Junger's account of *The Perfect Storm:*

GEORGES BANK, 1896

"One midwinter day off the coast of Massachusetts, the crew of a mackerel schooner spotted a bottle with a note in it. The schooner was on Georges Bank, one of the most dangerous fishing grounds in the world, and a bottle with a note in it was a dire sign indeed. A deckhand scooped it out of the water, the sea grass was stripped away, and the captain uncorked the bottle and turned to his assembled crew: 'on Georges Bank with our cable gone our rudder gone and leaking. Two men have been swept away and all hands have been given up as our cable is gone and our rudder is gone. The one that picks this up let it be known.'

The note was from the *Falcon*, a boat that had set sail from Gloucester the year before. She hadn't been heard from since. A boat that parts her cable off Georges careens helplessly until she fetches up in some shallow water and gets pounded to pieces by the surf. One of the *Falcon*'s crew must have wedged himself against a bunk in the fo'c'sle and written furiously beneath the heaving light of a storm lantern. This was the end, and everyone on the boat would have known it. How do men act on a sinking ship? Do they hold each other? Do they pass around the whisky? Do they cry?

This man wrote; he put down on a scrap of paper the last moments of twenty men in this world. Then he corked the bottle and threw it overboard. There's not a chance in hell, he must have thought. And then he went below again. He breathed in deep. He tried to calm himself. He readied himself for the first shock of sea."

Sebastian Junger, *The Perfect Storm*

Enter the Storm

Crews like the men on the *Andrea Gail* Men will take chances. Boats will start trips too late in the season, or stay out longer than planned if a trip is not profitable enough. The risks grow greater later in the season, since storms at that time tend to be more severe. This particular crew was in an unfortunate predicament. The *Andrea Gail* was filled with ice, but only about 20,000 pounds of fish—barely enough to break even. Supplies would run low if the boat kept fishing, and extra supplies and fuel meant greater costs—and less profit.

Like most fishing vessels of that time, the *Andrea Gail* received regular weather updates. Weather reports, received by radio or fax, were carefully scrutinized. When a boat is days out from shore, the consequences of poor judgment are literally life and death. On October 23, 1991, Billy Tyne and crew set their lines for what they knew might be the last run of the trip. Days later when Billy radioed a Canadian Coast Guard station, he had no idea of the ominous weather developments. Three large weather systems were on line to meet in the location where the *Andrea Gail* would soon arrive. Hurricane Grace had turned northeast from its Caribbean origin. At the same time, a storm system in the Great Lakes was moving east, and a Canadian storm to the north was moving south. All would meet in the unlikely location of the North Atlantic.

On the morning of October 27th, the *Andrea Gail* had entered Canadian territorial waters. The weather was still clear and the crew had no clue on what was happening around them. Storms arise quickly at sea, and Billy was concerned about weather reports faxed to him that evening. He spoke with another Captain, who agreed the weather patterns did not look good. Though no one can be certain of all the details, it appears the crew decided not to head to a port and ride out the storm. Meanwhile, meteorologists tracking Hurricane Grace watched with astonishment as the storm of the century developed. By the afternoon of October 28th, the beginning of the storm was upon the *Andrea Gail*. Conditions improved a bit that afternoon, but then the winds changed direction. By early evening the *Andrea Gail* found itself smack in the middle of the "perfect storm," a terrifying spectacle with monstrous waves up to 100 feet. Billy radioed the other boats in his fleet to say "She's comin' on boys, and she's comin' strong." It was the last message anyone would hear from the *Andrea Gail*.

The movie account of the *Andrea Gail's* last hours is a reasonable guess of what the crew encountered in that perfect and dreadful storm. Once the issue was life and death, we can be sure that anything on the boat was expendable. A lost boat and financial ruin would be irrelevant—even a relief—if they could stand on land again. Experienced fishermen fought for control, clutching the wheel, cutting lines, angling the boat—even as it made its roller-coaster ascent up the largest waves they had ever seen in their lives; larger, in fact, that anything they had even imagined or dreamt in their worst nightmares.

The Fate of the Andrea Gail

The decision to ride out a storm is a serious matter. Leaving a risky location for a safe harbor might mean the end of a trip and financial disaster. With so much on the line, a crew might disregard warnings that should be heeded. We can all relate to this kind of situation; it's convenient to believe that the dangers from terrible risks won't happen to us. Others may play the game and lose, but not us. At such times, we may be tempted to disobey the warnings of our instincts and experience. Money in particular has a way of clouding the picture.

The full details of Billy's fateful decision will never be known. While the crew certainly knew they were in for a bad storm, did they have any idea it would be the storm of the century? Did they debate whether it was worth the risk, knowing that once the decision was made, it would be too late to change course? When the screeching winds and monstrous waves struck with unimaginable fury, the men must have had the sickening realization that they made a mistake—literally, the worst mistake of their collective lives. Like so many before them at sea, the terrifying realization came: this is the day that I die.

The next day, families and friends back in Massachusetts got the terrible news. There was no radio contact with the *Andrea Gail*. For families and friends in this situation, hope doesn't perish in a day. A boat may have damaged its radio, or had some other problem that prevents contact. The days would stretch to agonizing weeks, punctuated with desperate phone calls seeking news. There would be searches with boats and planes, but the *Andrea Gail* would never be seen again. A few small parts from the boat would be found long after hope was abandoned, but the crew and boat were gone forever. The names of the crew eventually would be added to the somber bronze plaques in Gloucester, along with thousands of names of those who perished at sea, and almost as many forgotten stories.

A Spiritual Perfect Storm: The Story of Jonah

A storm at sea can be a terrifying event. For crews in centuries past, the sea was even more mystifying and threatening. Without modern means of detecting storms, there was no way to know when a tempest would strike—and how long it would last. Stories abound of ancient voyages in what would be small boats by today's standards. In fierce storms, sailors would throw their cargo and tackle overboard, forsaking profit for survival. In one intriguing story, during a particularly fierce storm, the crew threw a man overboard—*at the fellow's request!* Remarkably, the terrible storm that threatened the boat stopped immediately. The account does not tell the name of the boat, but it is a boat that I will call "Disobedience."

Why would someone ask to be thrown overboard during a fierce storm? You would imagine there must be a remarkable story behind such a request—and there is! The Bible records that remarkable story; it is the story of Jonah. The tale begins not with a boat, but an assignment from God to preach in the City of Nineveh. The great city was the capitol of the mighty Assyrian empire, located in modern day Iraq. From archaeological excavations we know the inner city was roughly three miles long by a mile and a half wide. Its massive walls may have reached one hundred feet, and were broad enough to accommodate chariot races around the eight mile circuit. According to the Bible, Jonah was sent by God to the city about the eighth century B.C.

But Jonah had other ideas. Rather than obeying the command, he defied God by running in what was figuratively *and literally* the opposite direction. Instead of traveling east to the city, he decided to board a ship and sail as far west as possible—to a destination called "Tarshish," the most distant land known at that time. What prompted Jonah's disobedience? Nineveh had a reputation for extreme cruelty, even by the standards of the ancient world. Contemporary drawings depict Assyrian armies mutilating their victims, and leading them captive by fishhooks. As an Israelite, Jonah probably had a patriotic dislike—or more likely, a patriotic hatred—for the brutal and relentless military machine working its way toward his homeland. God gave Jonah a simple message: *speak out against the wickedness of the city.* (Jonah 1:2)

By the end of the account we understand Jonah's reason for running from the assignment. In short, Jonah disobeyed God— and ran away—because he did not want the Assyrians to hear the warning. Jonah had a simple reason; if they heard, they might repent—and if they repented, God might not judge them for their cruelty. The disobedient prophet was not filled with the milk of human compassion for these people. He wanted the city to be judged, in whatever terrible form that might take. In fact, when Jonah finally (and reluctantly) preached to the city and it did repent, thereby avoiding God's judgment, he was upset! Here's what he said: *"O Lord, is this not what I said when I was still at home? That is why I was so quick to flee to Tarshish. I know that you are a gracious and compassionate God, slow to anger and abounding in love, a God who relents from sending calamity."* (Jonah 4: 2, NIV)

Get the picture? Jonah knew the character of God—loving, merciful, and compassionate—and he didn't want that interfering with the judgment he thought Nineveh so richly deserved. Essentially, Jonah believed he knew better than God what should happen to the Ninevites. In fact, God was not done with Jonah and would teach him a lesson about compassion and mercy. Jonah was not afraid of his assignment; far from it. He had a burning grudge, and it drove him to a boat that represented his disobedience to God's desires.

A Boat Called "Disobedience"

Jonah was a determined man. God had said "go to Nineveh," and so he decided to go as far as he could in the *opposite* direction; he was determined to disobey God. And the most effective way to do so was to board a boat headed to the port of Tarshish. Bible scholars generally agree that Tarshish was located in modern day Spain. The smaller boats of that day generally did not venture far into the great unknown expanse we now know as the Atlantic Ocean. Tarshish was the last stop on the line.

The account tells us that Jonah paid for his passage, much as people do to this day, though he also may have been assigned duties. We don't have any details on the size of the boat, the number of crewmen or the type of cargo. What we do know is that the boat ran into a terrible and fierce storm. The weather was so severe that the experienced crew feared for their lives. It seemed that the boat would be broken into pieces and all would perish. This is a drama common to people of all ages. Like the men on the *Falcon* centuries later, we wonder: how did they face death? Did they cry, or hug each other? Did they drink, or scream in anguish? Like the crew of the *Andrea Gail*, did they wonder: *is this the day I die?*

One human instinct in such terrifying times is turning to God. Desperate times cause us to rethink our convictions, demonstrated in the old adage there are no atheists in foxholes. After the crew threw all the cargo overboard to lighten the vessel, their thoughts turned to whatever god or gods they knew. As the Book of Jonah records it, everyone began to "cry out to (his) god." Everyone, that is, except Jonah. The disobedient prophet went below deck to the sleeping compartments to catch forty winks.

When the captain went below deck and discovered Jonah sleeping, he was incredulous. He roused the prophet to ask: *do you understand what's happening?* Every man on the boat was crying out to his "god," and Jonah had better start doing the same or they would soon be dead. Jonah's bitterness toward Nineveh had so desensitized him to the plight of others that he was able to sleep through the turmoil he had caused.

Despite all the steps of everyone on board, the storm grew worse; and no one's "god" was able or willing to help. The crew felt a growing sense of terror, which must have been evident on the faces of all. Like numerous generations of mariners before and after, the terrifying question burned in them: *is this the day I die?* Moved by this desperation, someone came up with a sensible thought for superstitious sailors: *a storm this ferocious is probably from an angry god; let's cast lots to see who is responsible.* Casting lots was something like throwing dice, and the finger of "chance" pointed at Jonah as the culprit. The crew frantically questioned him: *Who are you? What is your occupation? Where do you come from?* Most importantly they wanted to know: *did you offend your god and somehow cause this?* (Jonah 1:7-8)

Jonah was willing to tell all. He was a Hebrew, running from the God who had created the heavens and the earth, and the terrifying storm pounded them because of his disobedience. *What should we do to stop the storm,* they demanded. Jonah's solution was simple: since he was the cause of the tempest, throw him overboard, and the storm would end. Remarkably, the crew pitied Jonah, the prophet of God, more than he cared about them. At first the crew ignored his advice. Whitened hands gripped lines and rudder, fighting to control the boat, but nothing helped ... and the storm grew worse. Finally the terrified crew cried out to Jonah's God: *please don't hold this against us if it is this man's doing.* Then, the crew seized Jonah and flung him overboard. Their terror was soon mingled with awe and relief, for as soon as Jonah was out of the boat, the storm ended. Jonah would end up with far less comfortable surroundings for his return voyage. The biblical account tells how he was swallowed by some type of enormous sea creature and unceremoniously regurgitated on shore to go follow God's original instructions. (Jonah 1:12-17)

The point was effectively made; the once reluctant prophet picked the seaweed off his head and started on the long trek east to the city he despised. Nineveh would hear his message after all.

The Effects of Disobedience

As Jonah learned the hard way, getting out of a boat called *disobedience* may be much more difficult than getting in. God still speaks to us today about his desires for our lives, and the impact he wishes to have on others through us. We need the constant reminder that "it's not about me." This was the case for Jonah, for whom God had an urgent mission. Nineveh's great wickedness didn't lessen the call—in fact, it made it more pressing. God is not like an angry drill instructor waiting to swat us when we get out of line. He is a compassionate Father, urging us to repentance for our own good. And we are the instruments He uses to spread that message. God's purposes are intertwined with our love and concern for others; no man is an island.

We may try to run from God in our pursuit of disobedience, but the effort is futile. Where can we go to avoid his call to our minds and hearts? In short, there is nowhere we can hide from God. As Psalm 139 declares, *"Where can I go from your spirit? Or where can I flee from your presence? If I ascend into heaven, You are there; If I make my bed in hell, behold, You are there."* The psalmist was aware of God's presence everywhere because of a pressing inner awareness in his conscience. Conscience is never a matter of preference or opinion. It is a gift God has placed in us; a strong and brutally honest voice that speaks to us if we allow it. We can persistently try to ignore it, but we cannot deny its presence always at the edge of our thinking. Its urgency may be dampened through drugs or alcohol, or pushed aside by pleasure or fear, but somewhere and somehow it is never fully silenced. When we run from God it is a perpetual effort; we run in a circle and God's presence is at its center. Though Jonah attempted to run from the call of God, he could never escape the uncomfortably persistent voice pressing him.

Like Jonah, disobedience and ignoring the persistent tug of conscience will bring storms in our lives. And as Jonah's disobedience affected his companions on the boat, so will our disobedience threaten those on life's voyage with us. Defying God inevitably affects others, and can even bring destruction to those we care about deeply.

Have you ever wondered why God demands obedience? It is for our sake. Obedience is bound up with love—both God's love for us and His desire that we know and love Him. Jesus said it this way: "*If you love me, you will obey my commandments.*" (John 14:15) It is because He loves us that He pleads for our obedience, the way a father might urge his child with a new driver's license to follow traffic laws. Disobedience has consequences that love strives to prevent. This is why a God of love grieves over disobedience. The only path back is the determined decision to obey God and turn from our self will. We have to get out of the boat called "disobedience."

Getting Out of the Boat

Getting out of a boat of is always easier close to port. One can step on a boat, realize an error, and just as quickly turn and walk down the gangplank. As with disobedience to God, the sooner we come to grips and purpose to turn about, the less severe the consequences. Remaining on a course of disobedience takes us further from where we should be and makes the return course more challenging.

The case of Jonah is an interesting illustration of how disobedience works. Jonah knew that his disobedience had brought the storm that imperiled the life of all on the boat, and that the only hope for everyone was to get him off the boat. His advice was clear: *throw me overboard and all will be well.* If Jonah knew this, why didn't he simply jump off the boat? He was resigned to his fate, but unwilling to take the necessary step himself. I imagine the reason is that he was afraid, and needed the help of others. We may know the right course and wish to correct the mess we have made, but the needed steps may be difficult, even terrifying.

That's how it is when we wrestle with disobedience to God. Life's circumstances churn around us like a roiling sea, but it's just too hard to step away. We're paralyzed by the fear of consequences. What will people think? What will this cost me? How can I ever make it right? While we wrestle with these questions, the boat keeps moving, taking us further and further from where we should have been.

Have you found yourself on a course of disobedience for too long? Has the trip resulted in storms and turmoil for you and others? There is a way back, but it must start with getting out of the boat. Jonah asked others for assistance, and we should do so as well. Exiting the boat may be frightening and abrupt. It may take us from the shaky security of the deck into the churning waves. It is safer, though, to call on God in the ocean than it is to cling to the splintering deck of a boat called disobedience. As with Jonah, God is able to make a way in a dark ocean of helplessness.

Be willing to enlist the help of mature believers to help you out of the boat. We need the perspective and support of others whom we trust. Our eyes must see past the storm and accept the truth; there is no future on this boat. It will surely break apart some day, like the proverbial house built on sand. The joy of obedience to God can only come by getting out of the boat.

Here is an intriguing question: could Jonah have repented on board and simply caught the next ship back to Nineveh? If so, why did he suggest such drastic measures? It may be that Jonah *preferred* to die rather than obey God. How pathetic, and yet so very human! But, his ghastly "return voyage" brought suffering and gave him time to contemplate death. Perhaps the process of suffering awakened something in Jonah that led him to repentance. God's love is so deep and extraordinary that He will allow us to suffer, if that is what it takes to right the course.

Out of the Boat: A Life Transformed

The man in the ship was having a rough voyage. He had been rescued from another ship where he had been beaten, starved and shackled; even now he could recall the cruel leg irons biting into his flesh. He reflected on much of what he had seen in his life; of staggering cruelty, death, and lives sold cheap. Now on a ship called the *Greyhound*, he looked forward to reaching port and then returning home. As a sailor, he was accustomed to the hardships of sea, but the storm that awakened him that night was severe enough to worry him. As water began to fill the ship, the young man knew all aboard were in dire peril. In his mind the question formed as it did on other occasions in storms: *Is this the night that I die?*

On the occasion of this night, the man likely thought back upon his life of twenty-two years. He remembered his mother who had died when he was only six, and being shipped to boarding school afterward. In the few years of life he knew with his mother, one memory was vivid. His mother was a woman of faith, who prayed regularly for her small boy.

Perhaps with some pain he reflected on how he had run from that faith. He had gone to sea, like his father before him, and run from the Christian faith of his childhood. At the age of seventeen, while returning from a trip to Venice, he was pressed into naval service and was given the rank of midshipman. After deserting from the ship, he was recaptured, broken in rank to a common seaman, and placed in irons. Three years later, he pleaded to go on another ship, which happened to be engaged in the slave trade.

On the slave ship, the young man saw and did things he would never forget. He suffered through regular beatings, illness and starvation, though all his trials paled next to the fate of the human cargo in the hold of the ship—and he was part of their torment. For three years he endured the life of a slave trader, though he would later describe himself during these years with disgust and regret. At the end of three years he was rescued from the slave ship through the influence of his father. Now, aboard another ship headed for his home in England, the storm beating upon the boat and the storm in his tormented life merged into one event. Had he been saved from the cruelty of the slaver to perish on his way home? Was this a cruel cosmic trick, where his boat of deliverance was to become the instrument of his death?

The anguished young man had a sudden revelation. His life had been on a course of disobedience to the God he knew from watching his mother's life. The disobedience had brought terrible consequences. Now, he found himself in this storm, and the years of his life likely seemed empty and futile; here, possibly at life's end, what had his disobedience gained for him? And then the young man did something unexpected. In the distress of the storm, he called out to the God he had neglected for most of his life, reciting the Lord's Prayer. He would later say that on this night he sensed there was a God who heard and answered prayer. The young man afterward marked that day, May 10, 1748, as the time of his "conversion," and faithfully celebrated the day for the rest of his life.

After this anguished prayer, the weather miraculously cleared—just long enough for the ship to limp into port. The ship was terribly damaged, with so severe a list it could not have survived another storm. This close encounter with death profoundly changed the course of the man's life. He returned safely to England where he married and settled into family life. Certain changes in his life were immediately evident. He made efforts to curtail his swearing and much of his former lifestyle, except he remained in the slave trade and even rose in rank to captain a slave trader. It was only after he retired from the slave trade and entered the ministry that his eyes were fully opened to the evil he had participated in.

The Power of a Transformed Life

After leaving the slave trade, the man entered into the ministry, where he became acquainted with figures like Charles Wesley and George Whitfield. Yet, the truth of his former life and "occupation" weighed heavily on his conscience. Although he had turned from his disobedience to God, the effects of that disobedience had caused much harm to others. In a letter to a friend on October 21, 1775, he would write:

"You speak somewhere of 'atoning for disobedience by repentance.' Ah! my dear sir, when we are brought to estimate our disobedience, by comparing it with such a sense of the majesty, holiness, and authority of God; and the spirituality, extent, and sanction of his holy law, as he, and he only, can impress upon the heart of a sinner—we shall be convinced that nothing but the blood of the Son of God can atone for the smallest instance of disobedience!"

By now you may have guessed the man in this story is John Newton. Newton would go on to compose 270 hymns, though his best known and most enduring work would be the hymn that summarized his own life, *Amazing Grace*. There would be more to Newton's life, though, than the legacy of his writings and hymns. Newton would become a staunch abolitionist and mentor to a young man named William Wilberforce. William spent much of his teenage years in Newton's home, where he heard stories of the slave trade mixed with Newton's sermons. The passion of Newton's belief was caught by Wilberforce, who would then spend his entire life and political career fighting to end slavery in the British Empire. Wilberforce saw Parliament pass the Slavery Abolition Act in 1833, just three days before his death. The end of slavery in the Empire was in many ways a legacy to his mentor, Newton.

Though Newton became a beloved figure, he never lost sight of the deeds done in those terrible 23 years before his conversion. He wrote his own epitaph, which he thought a fitting summary of his life:

"John Newton, Clerk, once an infidel and libertine, a servant of slaves in Africa, was by the rich mercy of our Lord and Saviour, Jesus Christ, preserved, pardoned and appointed to preach the Faith he had long laboured to destroy."

The legacy of Newton's life is an encouragement to all of us in a boat called *Disobedience*. Mercy is freely available to those who, like Newton, call upon God in the time of their distress. A compassionate God does not ignore a truly repentant heart because it is awakened in a storm. In fact, it may be the very merciful design of God to place us in a storm, if that is what it takes to bring us to our senses and call upon Him.

Does God seem angry and unapproachable because of events in your life? The wonderful news is that He is not. He is waiting for you to decide you will get out of the wrong boat; and when you do, He will redeem the evil—just as he did for a "wretch" named John Newton.

Amazing Grace

Words by John Newton 1779

Amazing Grace! How sweet the sound
That saved a wretch like me!
I once was lost, but now am found
Was blind, but now I see.
'Twas Grace that taught my heart to fear,
And Grace my fears relieved.
How precious did that Grace appear
The hour I first believed.
Through many dangers, toils, and snares
I have already come.
'Tis Grace hath brought me safe thus far
And Grace will lead me home.
The Lord has promised good to me.
His Word my hope secures.
He will my shield and portion be
As long as life endures.
When we've been there ten thousand years
Bright shining as the sun,
We've no less days to sing God's praise
Than when we'd first begun.

CHAPTER FOUR: A BOAT CALLED DISCOURAGMENT

"It's no fish ye're buying, it's men's lives."
Sir Walter Scott
The Antiquary, Chapter 11

The Sultana

April of 1865 is a notable month in American history. It was in that month that President Abraham Lincoln was assassinated, General Robert E. Lee surrendered to Union armies at Appomattox, and the manhunt for John Wilkes Booth came to an end. Obscured by these well-known events was the worst maritime disaster in U.S. history: the explosion of the steamship *Sultana*. On April 27, 1865, at about 2:00 AM, a massive boiler explosion led to the death of more than 1,500 Union POWs on their way home.

The *Sultana* was a Mississippi River steamboat of the sort popularized by Mark Twain. Four boilers powered a newly-developed fire tube engine, which powered a giant paddlewheel. The *Sultana* had been built two years earlier at a cost of $60,000. She was 260 feet long and 39 feet wide, with an upper deck and officer's quarters. Her legal capacity was 376 people, though she was also built to carry an additional thousand tons of cargo.

At the conclusion of the Civil War, the Federal Government offered shipping companies a fee for every soldier they carried north on the Mississippi. The reward proved too strong a temptation for the boat's owners, who decided that filling every nook and cranny with soldiers trumped capacity restrictions. For its ill-fated trip, the *Sultana* was packed with Union POWs from the most infamous Confederate POW camps. As the South barely had enough food for its own armies, one can imagine the depravation and horrifying condition of the camps—on both sides of the conflict. Jim Walker gives the following account of the soldiers who boarded the *Sultana:*

"The 1,700-ton, two-year-old side-wheeler was jammed solid with at least twenty-three hundred people, well over twice her listed human capacity, plus more that fifteen hundred horses, cows, and pigs. The passengers had boarded her in Vicksburg, many of them hungry, ragged, sweating prisoners from the prison camps of Andersonville, Georgia; Macon, Georgia; and Cahaba, Alabama. Victory earlier that April had set them free. Their number was augmented by an overflow of soldiers from nearby Camp Fisk who struggled to obtain discharge papers and shoulder their way aboard."[1]

The broken and discouraged POWs had one burning desire—to get away from the nightmare of the prison camps to their homes as quickly as possible. Ship owners hired armed guards to keep the boisterous crowds from forcing their way aboard. The attempt to fill the boat was a raucous scene. Even as "Billy Yanks" struggled to get past the guards bayoneted rifles, the grizzled engineer, Nat Wintringer, puzzled over problems with the new experimental boiler. He and his assistant did what they could to plug some of the more obvious holes, but larger repairs would have to wait until the Sultana could get to a shipyard.

The cots inside the boat were dirty, smelly and tightly-packed. Despite this, accounts say that spirits raised as the boat began its trip north. However cramped and unbearable the conditions, they were on their way home. Jim Walker's colorful description of the ill-fated voyage gives details about individual passengers:

"Others like Otto Barden of Wooster, Ohio, were inhabiting gratings in recesses of the engine room despite the shattering noise, the grease, and the steam. Perhaps the heat acted as an anesthetic for Barden, who claimed the dubious distinction of having been captured by General Nathan Bedford Forrest's tough cavalry.

P.L. Horn, also of Wooster, defied the jungle of heads, arms, and booted legs to spread his bedroll on the top deck near one of the cinder-belching stacks. At least he obtained some night air, mingled with the soot and the sparks showering down upon him and his mates."[2]

At one point in the voyage the *Sultana* stopped in Helena, Arkansas. As a photographer set up his equipment to take a picture of the boat, the prisoners crowded to one side to get in the photograph. The uneven distribution of weight in the over-crowded boat nearly caused it to capsize, which would have been a mild fate compared to what was to come. You can see the actual photo in the photograph section of the book.

The Unforgettable Tragedy

After a brief stop in Memphis, the Sultana resumed her voyage on April 27th at about midnight. A light rain was falling. By the accounts of those in Memphis, who could see the flame-lighted horizon, the disaster struck at about 2:00 AM when most on the boat were sleeping. The initial blast of the boilers destroyed much of the boat and threw many passengers into the water. Immediately following the blast parts of the ship were engulfed in flames; passengers trapped in compartments would be burned to death before entering the river.

In the ensuing chaos, the boat sank slowly while people contended with the flames, the confusion, and the cries of those drowning around the stricken vessel. Passengers attempted to grab hold of floating debris, while fighting off the desperate grasping hands of those who could not swim. Accounts claim that a few on the boat, not fully recognizing the danger, urged remaining passengers to stay aboard while they maneuvered ashore. Estimates vary at the number who survived that evening, usually between 500 and 700. Whatever the actual number, an army surgeon treating the victims described their condition as "pitiable." By most accounts, more than half the survivors, many emaciated from their imprisonment, died within the next few months from a variety of maladies, burns, and exposure from the cold water. Somewhere between 1,600 and 1,800 people perished in the disaster that drizzly night—more than the approximately 1,500 who died on the *Titanic* or the nearly 1,200 on the *Lusitania*.

The Search for Answers

The exact cause of the explosion is still unknown, and official investigations reached no certain conclusions. To this day conspiracy theories remain about sabotage, or a bomb hidden in the boiler by Confederate spies eager to extract revenge on Union soldiers. The most probable explanation, however, is that the overcrowding caused or contributed to the disaster. One investigation found that the boat was top heavy, which caused it to list from side to side. With four interconnected boilers, the water ran out of the hottest boiler in the middle creating a dangerous hot spot. As water sloshed back from adjoining boilers, an enormous amount of steam would have been generated with no place to go. The intense buildup of steam pressure might well have caused the boilers to blow apart.

Whatever the cause, we know what drove desperate men to cram into every available part of the boat. Soldiers brutalized by the long war and terrible conditions of the POW camps were beaten and discouraged. Their burning desire was to get home, and the greedy boat owners, ignoring comfort and safety, were all too happy to oblige them. Discouragement will drive us to desperate acts, and desperate people will take chances. It also opens the door for others to take advantage of that desperation, in both the physical and spiritual realms.

A Man called Peter

What causes discouragement? Pulling the word apart is revealing: dis—couragement, or a loss of courage. We might think of discouragement as something like a loss of hope, or a sense of helplessness or powerlessness. While these are the *symptoms* of discouragement, it may be that the root is something like a loss of the courage that comes from uncertainty. Shattered confidence brings self-doubt, and a crisis of identity; discouragement is the outward manifestation of those shattered hopes and lost assurance.

With this in mind, we come to another story about one of the most remarkable characters in scripture: the Apostle Peter. Born with the name "Simon," the son of Jonah, Peter embodied all sorts of contradictions. He was a partner with James and John,

The Kursk

The Lusitania

Notice to Travelers
sailing in war torn waters

The Sultana

The Colborne
(not the actual colborne, visual representation)

The Andrea Doria

The Cyclops

The Dunkirk Evacuation

also destined to become apostles, in a successful fishing business. Peter was brash, self-confident, and a natural-born leader. He was rarely at a loss for words, and ready to throw out an opinion without much thought. Yet, he was capable of profound introspection and emotion, and impetuous and reflective in alternating turns. His encounter with Jesus transformed him from a boisterous fisherman to a leader of the first church in Jerusalem—and a source of encouragement to millions who would follow him. Before this remarkable transformation was completed, Peter would face the stripping away of his confidence and courage, and find himself in a boat of discouragement.

The Time of Certainty

Discouragement doesn't come when we feel confident about our beliefs and course of action. The first few years of following Jesus were a wonderful whirlwind and time of growing certainty for Peter. There were countless surprises; the blind were made to see and the deaf could hear. Lepers were healed, multitudes were miraculously fed, and the dead were raised. Even nature and the elements were at the Master's command. Moreover, Jesus' teaching was astonishing; the parables and images hinted at a wisdom they could barely fathom.

Over time, Peter emerged as a leader among the apostles, and one of the three intimates in the "inner circle." Moreover, when Jesus had asked *"Who do you say that I am,"* Peter had replied with certainty: "You are the Messiah, the Son of the living God."

"Blessed are you, Simon son of Jonah," Jesus replied, *"For flesh and blood has not revealed this to you, but my Father in heaven."* (Matthew 16: 13-17) Peter was riding high at that point! Jesus even gave him a new name: *Cephas*—the rock, or stone. This was heady stuff for a

gruff former fisherman; he was serving the Messiah, the Son of God. It was the time for the redemption of Israel, promised by the prophets of old. What could go wrong now?

The Prediction

The best of plans can unravel quickly, as Peter would soon discover. At what he likely thought the highest point of his life, he was destined to stumble over the stone of his self-assurance. The gospels record a poignant scene not long after Peter was dubbed "the Rock." At a solemn meal, the Master and Messiah told the disciples of his coming death, and the brief but terrible time in store for all of them. This did not fit with Peter's envisioned plans. So, in a flourish of over-confident certainty, Peter declared it would never turn out that way. "Even if everyone else fails you, I never will!" he thundered. I would wager he meant it, and would have passed a lie detector test. Peter would never forget the response to his swaggering certainty—"I tell you, before the rooster crows, you will deny three times that you even know me." (Luke 22: 33-34)

The rest of the story is well known. On the cold night of Jesus' betrayal, Peter would find himself seeking warmth at a fire with some of the crowd that had turned quickly and violently against his Lord. There were suspicious glances when others heard his Galilean dialect—wasn't that where this discredited prophet had come from? Were you with him, they demanded? Then, just as Jesus predicted, he denied that he knew Him—not once or twice, but three times. The third denial was angry and emphatic; the words were no sooner out of his mouth when the sound of the rooster crow split the pre-dawn chill. The dam of self-restraint and pretension burst, and Peter ran off into the darkness weeping. There was no more assurance, and with the loss of certainty came the loss of courage. He was shattered and distraught, and paradoxically, precisely where God wanted him. (Luke 22: 55-62)

A Boat Called Discouragement

We have all heard and said it: time heals. Acute emotional pain and obsession gradually fade like a receding tide, with waves of reminders. So it was with Peter. His emotional roller coaster would take him from despondency to amazement at an empty tomb, to elation at the resurrection, and back to shame over the memory of his failure and denial. Things were better, but they were not the same. Past boasting was a painful and mocking memory.

Peter had no way of knowing the role God had assigned him as a leader of the first Church, or the extraordinary route his life and ministry would follow. First, he would have to walk through the unmaking of his pride and confidence. As the Bible records it during this time, one day Peter turned to the disciples and simply said "I am going fishing." (John 21:3) We can easily miss the pathos of this comment. Jesus had said Peter would no longer fish in his beloved sea, but rather fish for men. Now, driven by the shame of his failure, he was back to the old, the comfortable, and the familiar. This was the place where he had cursed and fought, and toiled at his living. The comment revealed the depths of his discouragement, and the uncertainty of the disciples. They quickly agreed to go with him, to the old haunts and life; it was like the old times: they were going fishing. They were back on board the boat, but this time for a different reason.

If we are honest with ourselves, this is a temptation for all of us. We can listen to sermons or homilies ad nauseum, and have a pretty good idea of the ideal Christian life. We may know answers we can't seem to apply when struggling with life's issues. Sometimes we pray, and wait, and trust, and pray some more … and things get worse. There is built in all of us the desire to escape and engage in the old and familiar ways. Even when the old ways are destructive, there is a kind of comfort bred from familiarity.

Dave's Story

Dave, not his real name, was an old and dear friend. He had grown up in the streets of New York in the toughest of crowds. By his early teens he was seriously hooked on drugs and shooting heroin. His life was pushed by a sense of desperation; as he later described it, he did not expect to live long—so how he lived made no difference.

One day, as Dave listened to a friend and former addict speaking of Christ, something responded in his spirit. He had had enough, and wished more than anything he could break out of this horror he called life. At his friend's urging, he entered a Teen Challenge program and God got hold of his life.

Dave was a quick learner on spiritual life. His intelligence and the drive subdued by drugs returned; he entered Bible School and excelled. Soon he was heading a ministry, and regularly visited local jails where inmates packed his Bible studies. He was one of their own, a man from the street who had done time, and he spoke directly to their needs and emptiness. I went with Dave at times to watch his ministry. He was tough—a no-nonsense kind of minister—and very effective.

The ministry grew, and we attended fundraisers with glorious testimonies. Even local government officials saw how effective he was, and opened doors for further work. It looked like a marvelous work of God, until it came crashing down in tragedy.

Late one summer evening I got a call from Dave. My wife handed me the phone with a curious look; Dave was insisting he had to come see me immediately. It was a desperate matter, and he could not elaborate by phone. He was soon at our home and we settled into chairs on the deck, the welcome evening breeze providing relief from the day's heat. Dave was clearly bothered, though he seemed reluctant to speak. Then he abruptly slammed his hand on a table, startling me, and said with an anguished expression: *"I have AIDS."* The story unfolded in painful starts and stops, broken by my occasional questions. As his ministry was growing, his personal life was falling apart. His wife wanted him out of the house, and they fought constantly. His young son by a prior marriage was living in a terrible situation with his first wife and he was unable to get custody. The story poured out in torrents of pain; he had confided in no one and tried to get through it on his own strength.

Finally, he returned to old haunts and old friends. Like Peter standing at a fire on a cold Judean night, Dave had warmed himself at the wrong fire. He was seeking comfort in old and familiar places. Finally, one night with a group of old acquaintances, he shot up heroin again with a shared needle. That needle proved to be his undoing; it was that night he contracted *AIDS*.

In the nearly two years that followed until his death, I met with Dave on a regular basis and discussed things he had not spoken of with anyone. While he was able to make peace with God, he did not escape the consequences of his choices. The big question for me was: how? How did things get so far? How did his life unravel this way? The answers came in starts and periodic glimpses of self-realization. He was discouraged and weighed down by his sense of failure. Though he could put up a good front, he hid the hollow sense of futility and emptiness from nearly everyone.

Dave's decision to shoot heroin did not happen in a day; it was a slow decline. Discouragement left unchecked, drives us away from the God of hope. King Solomon would say it this way in Proverbs: "hope deferred makes the heart sick." (Proverbs 13:12) Just as the Apostle Peter had found comfort from the cold at a hostile fire, Dave had returned to the old and familiar for comfort. It was a fool's bargain; the old comfort was a sickly imitation of the new joy he had found—but it was better than nothing. He warmed himself at the fire of his old life with tragic consequences.

Getting Out of a Boat Called Discouragement

After denying Jesus, just as foretold, discouragement propelled Peter into his boat once again. It was not fishing for men—he may have wondered if he would ever do that—but it was comfortable and familiar. Befitting his frame of mind, the Gospel of John records his fruitless venture. Peter and his friends strained and worked all night, but caught no fish. The nets were as empty as the hollowness in his soul. (John 21:3)

As he sat in the boat with his friends, washing nets and tending to business, his eyes drifted to the shore. A distant figure was calling to them—trying to get their attention. The lone figure on the shore called to them: "Friends—do you have any fish?" Perhaps it was a hungry vagrant looking for a handout. They yelled back emphatically: "no." The stranger cried to them again:

"Throw your net out again on the right side and you'll find some." Although it was unlikely, they tossed the net hoping to pull in a small load. Instead, the net was so full of fish they couldn't drag it into the boat. (John 21: 4-6)

John stared hard at the figure on the shore. This was a familiar scene. Something like this had happened once before. And then it hit him; with excitement, he grabbed Peter and said: "It's the Lord!" A scene from years before must have come to Peter—of straining nets full of fish and snapping ropes, while he fell to his knees to say "leave me alone, for I am a sinful man." His excitement was too great to wait for the boat to work its way in. He plunged into the water to get ashore as quickly as possible—to be with Jesus who had just called to him.

The Power of Love

So what is it that gets us out of a boat of discouragement? It is, quite simply, the power of love. It is a love so profound that words cannot adequately capture it. In a moment, the revelation struck Peter. In all his fears and failures and in the pit of discouragement, Jesus stood on the shore calling him. God does not dwell on our failures, for His love sees us instead as He intends to remake us. It was a love so compelling that Peter could not remain in a boat drifting too slowly to shore. Love brings desire and eagerness to be with the one who loves us so fully and profoundly.

What was the turning point for the Peter in his struggle with failure and discouragement? I like to think it was the power of love, a love from which we cannot and do not want to hide. That love reached out to us when we were still at war with God; such love first transforms our perspectives and then our lives. Anger or strict rules may compel behavior for a time, but only love will win a heart and the deepest and truest allegiance. The Apostle Paul would express this beautifully in asking the Romans *don't you know it is the goodness of God that leads us to repentance?* (Romans 2:4)

Perhaps you find yourself in the grip of discouragement even as you read these words. Honestly examine what you are feeling behind the emotion. It's likely that, like Peter, you are weighed down by a sense of failure or inadequacy. Here is the wonderful news: we all share these feelings at times, but they can be precisely what God uses to show His love in a way we could have never otherwise experienced. Failure is not the end of the road with God; it is the platform for a clearer revelation of His love.

It may be hard to believe this, even as it was for Peter. Yet, it is precisely the case. In the paradoxical economy of God it is the poor in spirit who are blessed, and those who mourn who are happy. Our strength is nothing to God, but the scripture promises that *in our weakness* He will be strong in us. (2 Cor. 12:9)

The voice of God calls to us in the boat of discouragement, if we will but have faith to hear it and respond. Even now, in the grip of discouragement, turn your eyes to the shore where a solitary figure is calling out. See Him there as Peter did. Jesus knows every one of our missteps and denials before they happen, and intercedes for us. His unimaginable love sees no anger when we stumble, but instead joy over our restoration. No measure of failure on your part can keep Him from loving you. Hear it and believe it, and let it propel you from the boat of discouragement into the waiting arms of redemptive love.

CHAPTER FIVE: A BOAT CALLED DISTRACTION

"Nodding the head does not row the boat."
Irish Proverb

The Colborne

The wreck of the *Colborne* in 1838 off the coast of Quebec would have likely been one of the innumerable forgotten disasters at sea if not for Margaret Grant MacWhirter. In 1919, MacWhirter published a book[1] on navigating the Saint Lawrence Seaway in the 19th Century. Her account of *"The Wreck of the Colborne"* was drawn from traditions in the Province.

A character in the tragedy was Sir John Colborne, a man of means and a high ranking military officer. Colborne liked a high and elegant standard of living, which he thought fitting his rank. In keeping with his character, he had ordered an expensive silver collection from England, which was sent—by strange coincidence—on a vessel that bore his name. The *Colborne* was not a large vessel by the standards of that time, but for this particular voyage it was packed with expensive luxury items of the day, including wine and spirits, valuable whale oil, spices, and costly ornaments for churches. The ship was also packed with money—including gold to pay English troops stationed in Canada.

When the Colborne left London it carried 38 passengers and a crew of 17 men. Most of the passengers were from upper society, including military men traveling with their families. Among these was Captain James Elliott Hudson, traveling to Canada with his wife, five daughters and four sons. On the night of October 15th, forty five days after leaving London, the *Colborne* was at least nearing her destination. She would come close to the shore of Quebec, but not reach her destination intact.

Getting Off Course

One does not have to be a sailor to appreciate the dangers of getting off course. The smallest deviation literally starts a new course, and a variation off the deviation accelerates the process. Figuring out how it works is a fairly easy math problem. Someone traveling in a straight line that veers off by a miniscule 1 degree will end up about 900 feet off course in ten miles. A mistake of 6 degrees will put you off course more than a mile, assuming you make no further deviations after that. Traveling 50 or 100 miles with some minimal error of degrees will easily put you many miles off course, which could be the difference between safety and disaster.

That's why sailors (before modern computerized navigational aids) looked to a distant fixed point, or a point of reference. Going off course is not a problem so long as you have a view of a landmark and can make course corrections. This, of course, is the point of a lighthouse; it is, quite simply, a reference point in the dark. Its beacon guides ships from rocky coastline to a safe harbor. The failure of lighthouses, or severe fogs that hid the light, have caused innumerable disasters at sea. Perhaps less known is the phenomenon of false lights. Throughout history, enterprising criminal minds have lit lights to lure unsuspecting boats to the wrong destination. An old Alfred Hitchcock movie, *The Jamaica Inn*, tells the story of a group of pirates who lit large false fires on shore near dangerous reefs. Crews thinking they were on a safe course marked by the local lighthouse ended up crashing into the shoals, after which the pirates would murder the crew and passengers and then loot the ship. Navigating to a true fixed point, like sailing to the North Star, is critical in staying on course.

There's No such light...

Forty five days after leaving London, the Colborne had drifted off course. The boat should have been in the Gulf of St. Lawrence entering the Saint Lawrence River, which narrowed for several hundred miles leading to its destination, Quebec City. The correct course in the Gulf skirted past Anticosti Island, over one hundred miles long, sitting between Saguenay Province to the north and Gaspe Peninsula to the south.

For the sea-weary passengers and crew a relaxed atmosphere spread over the boat, now nearing its destination. The highly regarded guests and unusual amount of valuable cargo likely created a sense that there was something special about this voyage, though no one was unhappy over a safe ending. Land was in sight—a very good sign indeed. The problem was it was the wrong land. The boat had veered far south off course and was sailing near the rocky shore of the Gaspe coast. In the words of the Treasure Trove account, "...a fatal and inexcusable error had been made in the reckonings."

A survivor of the fatal voyage, Joseph Jones Acteson, recognized that the boat was far off course. He went to Captain Kent to warn of the error, but Kent insisted the light on the shore was coming from Anticosti Island. Acteson insisted that "no such light" was kept on the island, and that they were probably looking at Mount Anne on the Gaspe Peninsula, nearly one hundred miles off course to the south. Kent would hear nothing of it and dismissed Acteson's concerns. Captain Kent had seen a light, but the illumination was a false guide.

According to Acteson's account, at around midnight on October 15th, Captain Kent and Captain Hudson were having a glass of wine in the cabin. Suddenly, one of the ship's hands cried out "breakers ahead!" Before the ship could change course, the stern struck into rocks, crushing the rudder. Without a helm, or steering device, the boat was at the mercy of the sea.

By MacWhirter's account, chaos ensued quickly: "'In an instant the ship was a scene of wild confusion and distracting terror, the women and children fleeing from their berths to the cabin and some to the deck, sobbing and overcome with fright. The pumps were tried and eight feet of water was found in the hold." With no way to steer or maneuver the ship, the first mate asked for permission to cut down the masts and get the life boats ready. Compounding his error, Captain Kent made yet another blunder. "There is no danger," he insisted, and would not cut the mast poles. Instead, he gave orders to maneuver the sails to swing the boat away from the rocks, after which they could head to shore.

By shifting the sails, the crew was able to maneuver the boat into deeper water away from the rocks, but the boat was taking on water quickly; in a short time it would sink unless they could get to the nearby shore.

The Disaster

As the crew struggled in vain, the wind shifted again and blew the boat back toward the rocks. Only a half hour after the first strike, the boat smashed again into the rocks, this time turning over on its side. Passengers and crew were flung violently into the frigid waters, where most went under quickly. Six people managed to scramble into a life boat, but almost instantly a huge wave hit their boat, hurling them into the sea. One of the six, the passenger Acteson who had warned they were off course, managed to reach another life boat near the mast where he was joined by three crew members.

After clearing the boat from the ship's rigging, the crew members tried to rescue others in the water nearby, but were hampered by having no oars. Maneuvering was next to impossible in the choppy waves, and so the little boat drifted at the mercy of the sea. The boat managed to save two of Captain Hudson's sons, who were clinging to the rigging, but the rest of that long nightmarish evening would prove fruitless. With a few boards found in the boat, the crew was able to make a small sail, which kept them out in deeper water and prevented them from capsizing. Throughout the night, survivors clinging to pieces of the boat cried and wailed. The last moans of those in the frigid waters were heard until dawn, though the lifeboat was powerless to help any.

Of the fifty-five souls who boarded the boat in London, all but twelve perished. Most of he highly prized cargo, gold ornaments and silver plates, was lost to the sea. One young sailor who perished just before the dawn was one of those tragic ironies of life. Back in London, the young man ran up the dock and leaped on the *Colborne* just as it was pulling away from the dock. Had he arrived literally seconds later, he would have missed the voyage.

By 5:00 AM the next morning, local residents had become aware of the disaster and the survivors in the small boat were rescued. Eventually the remains of the *Colborne* were dragged into a cove, nearly two miles away. In the gruesome wreckage, bodies of passengers were found snagged in the rigging and debris. Other bodies were recovered from the water, and over the ensuing months many items were fished out of the ocean or washed ashore.

The danger of getting off course applies to more than travel at sea. On the early morning of August 31, 1983, Korean Air Lines (KAL) flight 007 was ready to take off from Anchorage, Alaska. The plane had stopped to refuel on its trip from NY City to Seoul, Korea. Just after 4:00 AM local Alaska time, the plane roared down the runway, intending to traverse the North Pacific on a course over Japan, and then on to Korea. None of the 269 occupants on the commercial airliner suspected they would not live to see another day.

Shortly after taking off, the plane veered very slightly off course westward. Anchorage's high frequency navigational system was out of order that night, and the plane was relying on its autopilot system set to the magnetic north pole. About ten minutes into the flight, the plane first deviated from its intended course. After twenty minutes, the plane was 5.6 nautical miles (NM) off course, and at fifty minutes out, military radar at King Salmon, Alaska, tracked the plane at 12.6 NM deviated. One by one, KAL 007 plunged through checkpoints, each registering the growing deviation off course and on a route that would take it hundreds of miles off course and over Soviet airspace.

At three hours, the ill-fated plane entered Russian territory, north of the City of Petropavlovsk, on course to fly over the large Island of Sakhalin off the coast of Russia. Much of the world was unfamiliar with the barren, elongated island, but that would soon change. Soviet air defense had been tracking the flight for over an hour since it first entered Russian airspace. When the plane, now thought to be a possible spy craft, reentered Russian territory over

Sakhalin, military jets were sent to intercept it. One jet fighter who later defected to the West claimed he fired warning shots, though he admitted it was unlikely they could be seen. Finally, the jets were ordered to bring down the craft before it could return to international waters. The lead fighter fired two missiles that found their mark. The pilots on KAL 007 struggled to control their wounded craft to no avail; the airliner began a death spiral, finally crashing on Moneron Island.

President Reagan would later characterize the attack as a "massacre," and Cold War tensions flared. The world was brought to the brink of an international crisis, originating with a plane drifting slightly off course.

Distraction

The Colborne and KAL disasters dramatically demonstrate the danger of drifting off course. Obviously, straying off a planned route is not always the result of distraction; the ill-fated KAL flight was the victim of something like equipment failure. While other factors certainly can pull one off course, distraction is one of the most common sources of navigational error.

Webster's 1828 dictionary says the root of the word "distract" is literally to "pull apart," or "to pull in different directions and separate." In elaborating on "distraction," Webster uses synonyms like "confusion," "madness," "disordered reason" and even "folly in the extreme." Distraction is a picture of someone attempting to move in two different directions simultaneously. Only one direction wins, and hence distraction is a picture of moving in the wrong direction.

Of all the boats in this book, distraction is perhaps the most challenging to recognize. The problem with distraction, in fact its very nature, is its subtlety. The thing that distracts us may not necessarily be bad. In fact, it may even be good or necessary in another context; but it is not what we should be doing at the time. It may even result from complacency or force of habit. Distraction makes us ineffective by confusing our priorities and diverting us onto the wrong track. Over time, that course deviation can be disastrous—for a boat, a plane, or a life.

A Boat Called Distraction

As (Jesus) walked by the Sea of Galilee, He saw Simon and Andrew his brother casting a net into the sea; for they were fishermen. Then Jesus said to them, "Follow Me, and I will make you become fishers of men." They immediately left their nets and followed Him.

When He had gone a little further from there, He saw James the son of Zebedee, and John his brother, who also were in the boat mending their nets. And immediately He called them, and they left their father in the boat with the hired servants, and went after Him.

Mark 1:16-20

At first glance, the activities taking place in a boat called distraction may not seem like a bad thing. Certain actions are harmless enough in themselves, or maybe even good. As one example, John's gospel records the story of two sisters, Mary and Martha. These women and their brother, Lazarus, were close friends of Jesus. They had him in their home on multiple occasions, and it was a place where Jesus seemed able to relax. Of course, wherever Jesus went crowds followed. Everyone wanted to see and hear the prophet from Galilee—and guests in the house meant cooking and serving. On one occasion, while Mary sat listening to Jesus, Martha was stuck doing all the serving. As her frustration built, she likely banged pots and scowled at her sister to make a point. Finally the long-suffering Martha could stand it no longer. "Master," she chided, "tell my sister to help me serve." (Luke 10:40)

It's easy to see Martha's point and even sympathize with her. Shouldn't everyone share in the work? Jesus' unexpected reply puzzles us even today; "Martha, you are worried about many things, but Mary has chosen the better course and it will not be taken away from her." (Luke 10: 41-42) Did Martha do something wrong? Clearly she did not. Could Martha have been doing something *better*? Yes; sitting at the feet of Jesus to hear his words. Serving the guests was a good thing, but a distraction from the best course. When distraction takes us off course it may seem a little thing at first. Over time, a minor change of direction turns into a new course—and maybe a new destiny. Little decisions of the moment become momentous decisions over the course of a life.

A minister friend named John tells a story about visiting an old western town with his family. They were strolling down the dirt main street, shoes kicking up puffs of dust, and admiring the authentic-looking hotel and saloon. John's attention was suddenly caught by a glint of light in the dust. Bending over, he scooped up a small copper colored bb. The little spherical shiny ball fascinated him for some reason. Then, his eye caught another and he picked it up as well. The area was filled with these bbs—the aftermath of a mock gun battle. His eyes strained and scoured the dirt as his family moved on and rounded a corner. Here was another, and another, and soon his cupped hand was filled with bbs, clattering as he shook his hand to get a better feel for his treasure.

The minutes rolled by until he looked up and realized his family was gone. They had gone to watch the cowboy show—the very reason for the trip—and John had missed most of it. When finally reunited with his family everyone wanted to know: *where were you?* The only answer he could give was to stick out his hand and show what he had been doing. As he did so, the thought struck him. He had invested almost an hour of his life in an activity, missed most of a cowboy show, and what did he have to show for it? Only a handful of bbs.

Getting Out of a Boat Called Distraction

Distraction does not necessarily come from activity; in some cases it may even come from idleness. The essence of distraction for John at the cowboy show, however, was a wandering mind and busy hands. Left unchecked, it kept him from something better. This was the same danger for the apostles James and John in Mark's account of their call to follow Jesus. When Jesus came to call them to join him they were sitting in a boat on the shore, mending their fishing nets. Their hands were busily repairing tears in ropes, fixing holes, and removing debris. It was a necessary thing for fishermen—even a good thing—but not the best course for their life. When Jesus called to them, they instantly dropped what was in their hands, rose up, climbed out of the boat and followed the teacher down the dusty path away from the shore.

Imagine for a moment if James and John had heard Jesus call to them and decided they needed to fix the nets first. It's not a difficult thing to imagine. Their father was nearby, and they surely wanted to show a proper respect for him and diligence towards the family business. "Master," they might have said, "keep going while we finish fixing these nets. We'll catch up with you later— maybe in town somewhere…" Would the chance have come again if they had delayed in responding?

Delay may be a symptom revealing an inner lack of commitment, or even what the Bible sometimes calls a "divided heart." Luke's gospel records a story where Jesus said to an unidentified man nearly the same words: "Follow me." The man responded "Lord, let me go first and bury my father." Jesus' response was short and to the point, maybe even a little harsh sounding to our modern ear: "Let the dead bury their own dead, but you go and preach about the kingdom of God." (Matthew 8: 21-22) The man's response to Jesus has to be understood in light of the customs and speech of that time. It might sound as if the man's father had just died and he wanted to attend the funeral, but that is not the gist of his request. The expression is better understood to mean the man wished to stay at home and tend to family needs and business until his father passed away; then, he would be free of obligations and ready to serve God. It was the distraction—of family needs, or life's circumstances and demands. Jesus was not advocating irresponsibility, but rather the pressing truth that the call of God does not wait. If we delay answering the call to get circumstances more favorably aligned, we risk getting derailed and missing the will of God in our lives. This is the great danger of distraction.

How did the brothers James and John get out of a boat of distraction? *By putting down what was in their hands.* The hardest part of exiting this boat is not something obvious, like the raging storm in Jonah's case. It is not physical effort so much as mental clarity needed to say: *I have to stop doing this thing that distracts my focus.* Getting out of a boat of distraction is a decision, heeding the penetrating voice that disrupts our routines and complacency, urgently whispering *there is something more than this.* The object of distraction is rarely a bad thing in itself; truly bad desires are usually obvious to us. We generally do not commit an assault or theft from distraction, but rather from anger or envy. The harm of distraction is not in the sudden blow that shatters, but in the slow corrosive effect through which the best is lost. Distraction numbs us and brings a loss of focus, and we stray bit by bit off a true path into barren land.

What does a boat of distraction look like in everyday life? How can we tell when we are off the mark, and missing the will of God in our lives? Countless inspired writings have not exhausted the topic, and no short treatment here can begin to do it justice. A few simple questions, though, may help start the process of identifying distraction.

First, is there something you believe God has called you to do that you have put aside until you feel *ready*? Preparation is a good thing, but not when it leads to paralysis. There are some areas in life where we simply have to plunge in and obey the call. If we think of all the things we must get done first, we run the risk of becoming the man who said to Jesus *"Let me go first and bury my father."* Let the dead bury the dead and heed the call.

Second, do you experience a deep and hidden joy in how you serve? The hidden inner joy is a promise of God to those who obey him—who keep his commandments. Jesus said *"If you keep my commandments, you will remain in my love, just as I have kept my Father's commandments and remain in His love. These things I have told you so that my joy may remain in you and your joy may be full."* (John 15: 10-11) When we obey God's desires for our lives, we will feel the joy of fulfilling our purpose—of doing what He designed us to do. If we do not experience that joy, it may be a sign we are distracted from the call. This joy does not depend on results, the praises of others, or worldly recognition. It is instead a deep inner joy that is not lost by changing circumstances. It comes from *obedience* to God; distraction that pulls us off the course absorbs our time and energy, and robs our inner joy.

Third, was there another time when you felt a greater passion for God? If so, what has changed? God certainly has not, for He cannot change His nature. If something has changed *it has been on our part*. There is a story about an older married couple driving in the family car. The wife looked out her window thoughtfully and then across the bench seat to her husband. "We used to sit close together in this car when we were first married" she said with a sigh. Her husband glanced over and replied "I haven't moved." Like the husband in the story, the eternal God hasn't moved. Think back to the time of that greater love and passion for God and prayerfully ask Him to show you where you may have strayed off course. The smallest decision or compromise is, in reality, the start of a new course. There is a point on the horizon—a bright light that cannot be mistaken—and heading back toward it is the beginning of the process of restoration.

The Key to Staying on Course

The smallest decision is, in reality, the start of a new course. If we do not lift our eyes to the horizon and navigate our course to a fixed point, we will be at the mercy of whatever circumstances lie on the wrong course. For a follower of Christ, the fixed point on the horizon has been told to us. Jesus said it plainly enough, even if our modern thinking does not fully grasp the significance of the words. To be his disciple, Jesus said each of us must engage in a *daily* course of denying ourself, picking up our cross and following him. (Matthew 16:24) It's a decision and action taken *every day*, repeated through our lives. *Denying ourselves* means surrendering our will to Him, foregoing our own desires to obey his commands. *Picking up our cross* is even more startling. His audience understood it clearly enough; it was a call to die, or death to self. The more modern equivalent would be to say take your noose or electric chair. Finally, there is the call to *follow*. It is motion—the course of life—with an eye on the goal. If we take our focus off the cross, or follow a false light, we will be at the mercy of an unknown path and destiny.

By studying the disasters of the Colborne and KAL 007, we learn important lessons about drifting off course. The way to stay on course is *seeing the fixed point or landmark and heading toward it continually.* In the case of a boat traversing dangerous and dark waters, the point is a lighthouse. It is a fitting and illuminating (no pun intended) example for life application. A beacon of light illumes what would otherwise be dark and treacherous waters.

But there are two types of light that may illuminate our course, and one is as dangerous as the absence of light altogether. This is the deception of false light. Whether we follow it mistakenly, as Captain Kent on the Colbert, or through treachery, like that of the pirates in *Jamaica Inn,* it leads to disaster.

False Lights and the True Light

Mariners throughout the ages navigated to one universal reference that was as certain—even more certain—than any on land. In times before electronic equipment and modern techniques, that unwavering friend of sailors was the North Star. Whenever it was visible, mariners of old learned how to sail under its guidance. However, it was not simply the location of the North Star that made it valuable; it was its location *in relation to the lesser stars.* There was a place in navigation, one might even say a *need,* for other lights—but only to serve as reference points to the guiding beacon called the North Star.

This makes an interesting picture for our lives. We all have other "lights" in our view; we may call them names like family, employment, pleasure, or even religion. Within the cluster, though, is there something you follow as a North Star? It is the one thing you believe to be true in making decisions on how you will live; it is the fixed point toward which you orient your life. We all make errors, but mistakes are ultimately acknowledged by evaluating our actions against what we believe to be true. In other words, if we think we have "strayed," it is from something we believe and accept as truth. The ultimate truth you believe, as more important than all other beliefs, is your North Star. Do you see a North Star in your life? Try to put a name to it right now as you read this. What is the one thing you believe to be fixed and true no matter the circumstances? Once you have it in mind, the next question becomes vital for all of us. Are we orienting our lives around the true light, or a lesser and *false* light?

We should also consider whether we have accurately identified the "light" we follow. If, for example, we claim a faithful and loving God is our light, *do our actions match the claim?* Does the course of our life support the assertion? Do our priorities line up with what we say?

The Light of the World

There are all too many false lights in this world. Remember, the Bible warns that Satan himself is able to appear as an angel of light. (2 Cor. 11:14) In truth, most people follow lights we know all too well. They are lights of money, power, influence, possessions, prestige, self, and a hundred others. When we travel through life with our eyes on such a false light, all that we do, every way we conduct ourselves, is oriented toward that goal. Yet, according to Jesus, the life spent in pursuit of any one of these has lost sight of its correct eternal goal. It is precisely what He spoke of in saying: *The one who seeks to keep his life in this world will lose it, but the one who loses his life for my sake will find it.* (Luke 17:33) No matter how much or what we achieve, this life ends—with all the promise or terrifying consequences of that reality. The words of martyred missionary Jim Elliott capture this profoundly: *He is no fool who gives what he cannot keep to gain that which he cannot lose."*

But there is in this world the promise of a true light—a North Star by which we can navigate in life. Fittingly, Jesus used this very image to describe himself. He would say: *I am the light of the world"* and *"He who follows Me will not walk in darkness, but have the light of life."* (John 8:12) One of his followers would say this of Him: *"(He) was the true light which gives light to every man coming into the world."* (John 1:9) On another occasion Jesus made this promise: *"This is the judgment of the world, that the light has come into the world, and men loved darkness rather than light, because their deeds were evil. For everyone practicing evil hates the light and does not come to the light, lest his deeds be exposed. But he who lives in truth comes to the light…"* (John 3: 19-20)

He is truly the light of the world and a lighthouse to keep us on course through the voyage of life. Let His words and demands shine as your beacon in dark and uncertain waters. No matter how terrifying or uncertain the place we occupy, we are always moving in some direction. Resolve to ignore the lesser lights and deny the lure of false lights. The true light of the world is the Son of God, and any other course puts us in peril.

CHAPTER SIX: A BOAT CALLED DISRUPTED PLANS

"The cure for anything is salt water—sweat, tears, or the sea."
Isak Dinesen

"The wonder is not that the Andrea Doria sank, but that she stayed afloat so long."
Leonard J. Matteson
United States Maritime Law Association

The Andrea Doria

Not all boat disasters end up with a terrible large-scale loss of life. One of the best known boat disasters of modern time saw a courageous coordinated effort that rescued 1,660 passengers and crew, even though half the lifeboats on the ship were useless. This is the story of the *Andrea Doria.*

Following World War II, the economy of Italy was in shambles. Although the nation had switched sides before the end of the war, allied nations still demanded war reparations. The scarred countryside bore testimony to the devastation of the conflict, with numerous cities and once beautiful landmarks ravished. Nearly half of the Italian merchant fleet had been destroyed during the war, and infighting in post-war governments made economic recovery more challenging. In the early 1950s, in an effort to reestablish national pride, the Italian Line produced two magnificent state-of-the-art ships. One of these was the *Andrea Doria*, named after a sixteenth-century Genoese admiral.

The ship was 697 feet in length and could hold 1,200 passengers and a crew of 500. She was designed and built with all manner of safety features including a double hull and eleven watertight compartments, any two of which could fill without the ship sinking. The *Andrea Doria* also boasted the most modern radar system of its time, making it one of the safest ships ever built to that date. Beyond the design marvels, the ship's most notable feature was its luxurious decor, which in places bordered on opulence. She was the largest, fastest, safest and most beautiful of all the ships in the Italian fleet, or as an Italian travel poster described it: "(The) greatest, latest and fastest Italian liner." Thus dubbed, the pride of the fleet was officially launched on June 16, 1951, though her maiden voyage would not occur until January of 1953.

Early Warning Signs

Though luxurious and fast, the *Andrea Doria* had certain design issues. Model testing during the design phase revealed a tendency to list after, or tilt to one side, when struck by a significant force. The effect was actually observed when the completed ship was hit by a large wave, and empty fuel tanks exaggerated the problem. This lack of stability would be addressed in the post-sinking investigation, particularly since the list (or tilt) after being rammed rendered the lifeboats on one side of the ship unusable.

An actual photo of the ship sinking, seen in the photograph section, gives an idea of the challenge in the rescue effort.

On the ship's maiden voyage, while off Nantucket Island, a large wave careened into the vessel, causing a list of about 28 degrees—severe by sailing standards. A list of more than 20 degrees allowed water to flow from one airtight compartment below into an adjacent compartment, compounding the risk of sinking when the ship took on water. Despite these design issues, the maiden voyage was completed in record time. The *Andrea Doria* would make one hundred trans-Atlantic voyages, nearly all filled to passenger capacity, before its fateful trip ending on July 25, 1956.

A Collision in the Fog

As evening fell on July 25th the *Andrea Doria* coursed westward, nearing the Massachusetts coast. She was scheduled to dock the following morning in New York. As she entered thick fog near the coast, Captain Piero Calami reduced speed and took customary precautions for reduced visibility. Meanwhile, a smaller Swedish liner, the *MS Stockholm*, was cruising eastbound in the same heavily-traveled ship corridor. With heavy fog looming in its path, *Stockholm's* crew had no view of the approaching *Andrea Doria*. Even with the *Doria's* reduced speed, the ships were converging with a combined velocity of 40 knots, or about 46 MPH.

Though visual contact was limited, both ships detected the approach of an oncoming vessel through their respective radar systems. What happened next was a remarkable error of miscommunication. As would be determined in safety hearings after the crash, each boat misinterpreted the other's course.

Without any radio communication, the *Andrea Doria* steered to port (or left, for landlubbers) intending a starboard to starboard passing. Simultaneously, the *Stockholm* veered starboard, intending a port to port passing. The actions timed together placed the ships on a hideous collision course.

By the time visual contact was finally made in the dense fog it was too late to avoid a collision. In a desperate last minute maneuver, the *Stockholm* reversed propellers, attempting to stop, and cut hard to starboard. At the same time, the *Andrea Doria* veered hard to port in a last-second attempt to avoid impact. Instead, the maneuvers caused the impact at nearly a right angle, with the *Andrea Doria* taking the worst part of the collision. Evasive maneuvers by the *Doria* only served to further expose its keel[1], making it more vulnerable to the coming blow. The steel — reinforced bow of the *Stockholm*, used for ice-breaking, tore into the *Doria* just below the bridge between watertight bulkheads. It also pierced and penetrated several passenger cabins, killing over 40 unfortunate passengers.

Because the *Stockholm* rode much lower in the water than the larger *Andrea Doria*, the resulting gash was closer to sea level. Sea water rushed into the shorn compartments, sealing the fate of the pride of the Italian line. The gash pierced five fuel tanks, filling them with tons of sea water. As the *Doria* took on water it listed severely—about 18 degrees—to the starboard side. The sickening tilt was close to the threshold at which water would flood adjacent compartments, dooming the vessel.

The two ships interlocked for about 30 seconds before slowly disengaging. The *Stockholm* had cut all its engines, but the *Andrea Doria* drifted forward into the fog, causing the demolished front of the *Stockholm* to further scrape and gash the *Doria's* side. As tons of water rushed in to the wounded ship, the *Doria's* crew pumped water to counteract the flooding. The maneuver backfired because of the severe list and actually worsened the problem. Over the next few minutes the list increased to the critical 20 percent mark and then beyond. Captain Calami realized that the ship could not be saved, and his job was to save as many passengers as possible. It was time for the lifeboats and an SOS signal.

The Evacuation

The decision to evacuate all passengers and abandon the *Andrea Doria* was made within 30 minutes. However, one glaring problem was immediately evident. Although the ship had enough lifeboats to carry all aboard, the boats lining the port side were unusable. The severe list left them too high above the water level for a safe launch. The starboard boats were usable, but could not be launched without difficulty, again, owing to the severe list. Compounding this problem, hundreds of injured passengers sprawled around the ship, some trapped in the wreckage, while the list steadily grew more severe. As if this was not sufficiently challenging, reports claim that many of the crew abandoned the ship first on the most accessible lifeboats. Without most of the crew to supervise, panic quickly set in. The rescue effort would be daunting, to say the least.

Meanwhile, the *Stockholm* had been spared from the *Doria's* fate. Though its front end was mangled and crushed, emergency steps stabilized the boat and kept her afloat. After determining his ship was in no danger of sinking, *Stockholm's* captain sent most of the vessel's lifeboats to the ailing *Doria*. The lifeboats ferried

Doria's passengers back to the *Stockholm*, though the crew was horrified to see the first three boats return with crew from the *Doria*. Afterward, passengers bitterly recalled the cowardly actions of the crew and the unnecessary panic caused by their abandoning the ship first.

Fortunately for the rest of the passengers, emergency calls sent out were quickly heeded. Ships in the area converged on the location and sent their lifeboats to aid in the rescue. The turning point in the rescue was the arrival of the French liner, the *Ile de France*. The French liner, which had passed the *Doria* earlier, turned around and arrived at the scene less than three hours after the collision. Almost miraculously, the fog at the scene lifted as the French liner arrived, allowing it to move close to the stricken vessel without danger. Its presence, with all exterior lights blazing, encouraged the stricken passengers and restored a sense of calm to the rescue effort. With many lifeboats now involved in the rescue operation, the evacuation proceeded speedily. In all, 1,660 passengers and crew were rescued and survived, though 46 persons perished as a direct result of the collision.

By daybreak, the evacuation process was complete. The last person to leave the stricken ship was Captain Calami, accompanied by crew members more honorable than those who had fled in the first lifeboats. The evacuation was finished by daybreak, an almost miraculous achievement thanks to the small fleet of lifeboats ferrying from other ships. The loss of life, except for a few injured evacuees, was limited to those who perished on impact.

One miraculous story of survival was that of 14 year-old Linda Morgan. Morgan was a passenger on the *Doria* in a compartment near the crash site. Somehow, the impact hurled her off the ship onto the deck of the *Stockholm*, where she was later found with no serious injuries. Sadly, her half-sister, Joan, who had been sleeping in the same cabin with her, was killed by the impact that propelled Morgan to the deck of the *Stockholm*.

The Sinking of the Andrea Doria

After the evacuation of the passengers and crew, thoughts turned immediately to whether the *Doria* could be salvaged and towed to port. The ship continued rolling on its side like a dying behemoth, slowly slipping below the surface as the damaged compartments flooded. It was soon evident to all the ship could not be rescued. By 10:00 AM, the *Doria* had rotated fully on its side, level with the horizon. Within ten minutes it slipped beneath the sea, forever lost. Some of the unusable portside lifeboats snapped free, floating eerily upside down above the spot where the ship slipped into its watery tomb. It was almost exactly eleven hours from impact to sinking. Evacuating the passengers and crew had been a race against time, a battle against the relentless list that complicated rescue and eventually capsized the ship. Thanks to the response of other ships in the area, the rescue effort succeeded and prevented an even greater tragedy.

A CBS News correspondent, Douglas Edwards, circled the area in a small plane as he described the scene. His words powerfully captured the pathos of the *Doria's* death:

There below, on glasslike water, water strewn with wreckage and oil, was the Andrea Doria, listing at a 45-degree angle and taking water by the minute ... the ugly gash in her side covered by the Atlantic... . Her three swimming pools were empty of water, emptied the hard way, spilled into the ocean.... A few minutes past ten o'clock ... the ship's list was at 50 degrees. Her funnels were taking water ... the boiling green foam increasing.... Three minutes later the Andrea Doria settled gracefully below the smooth

Atlantic—a terrible sight to see. A Navy commander had tears in his eyes. Nobody felt anything but an awful helplessness. There was one thing to be thankful for: the loss of life was not nearly, not nearly as great as it might have been. At 10:09 it was all over, the Andrea Doria was gone.

As with the "unsinkable" Titanic, there is tragic irony in the account of the Andrea Doria. Not many people know the Doria, with her state of the art safety equipment, was also dubbed "unsinkable." [2] She was built and designed to withstand a powerful impact and equipped with the best radar system in the world. Unlike Titanic, she was close to land and traveling in warm waters; but in the end was undone by simple human error.

Another Boat With Disrupted Plans

The Bible tells a story about another disastrous voyage with a successful passenger evacuation. As in the *Doria* account, some of the crew tried to sneak off first in the vessel's only lifeboat. Their plan failed when a passenger, who predicted the ruinous voyage, warned their escape attempt would bring a terrible loss of life. The captain heeded the warning and cut the lifeboat loose, while the passengers and crew fearfully awaited the voyage's outcome. Such was the remarkable voyage of the Apostle Paul on a ship bound for Rome. The voyage would end in shipwreck on the modern day Island of Malta with a mass evacuation but no loss of life. It was a voyage of disrupted plans, to put it mildly.

Travels of the Apostle Paul

The Apostle Paul traveled much of the known Roman world throughout his ministry. During the four "missionary journeys" mentioned in the Bible, he and his companions often traveled by boat. He was certainly no stranger to the dangers of journey by sea. About halfway through his ministry years, he wrote to Christians in Corinth that he had been shipwrecked three times and spent a full day and night drifting at sea. (2 Cor. 11: 25-26) Not all his voyages were so harrowing, but dangerous enough for him to claim he was "frequently in peril at sea."

One notable voyage takes up a full chapter in the Book of Acts. The story of the voyage begins with a trial where Paul, a Roman citizen, was stuck in a kangaroo court. His judge, a Roman territorial governor named Festus, wanted Paul to return to Jerusalem for a further hearing. Festus asked this, unaware that a band of men had vowed to kill Paul on the trip. Paul knew of the trap, and so instead of going exercised his citizen's right to have his case heard by the Roman Emperor. Festus was surprised by the request, since it meant a long and arduous journey to Rome. With a resigned shrug, he proclaimed: *You have appealed to Caesar? To Caesar you will go!* (Acts 25:12)

So began the voyage described by Paul's traveling companion, the physician Luke, in Acts chapter 27. Paul was among a number of prisoners bound for Rome, under the supervision of a Roman centurion named Julius. Sailing west from the coastal City of Caesarea, the first leg of the journey went smoothly. Following a change of ship at the City of Myra, on the southern coast of modern Turkey, Paul's boat continued cruising west and then veered south to the Island of Crete. It had been slow sailing to this point; with contrary winds from the west, the trip had taken many days more than planned. By hugging the shore and using the island as a shield, the boat barely managed to get to the port of Fair Havens—a harbor midway on Crete's southern coast. The boat's trials were just beginning. (Acts 27: 1-8)

The Decision to Press On

Now docked at Fair Haven, the boat's owner faced a difficult decision. Luke explains that the "Fast" was already over, which most scholars take as a reference to the *Day of Atonement*. According to ancient sources, the best season for sea travel was during the summer months, ending around mid-September.[3] Travel was possible but dangerous and unpredictable from mid-September through mid-November, and then ceased until spring. Winter brought shorter days with less daylight, fierce winds, poor visibility and even the possibility of snow. Since the feast was celebrated on tenth day of the seventh month of the Jewish calendar, it was now late September or early October—well into the dangerous sailing period. Wintering in Crete was the safe course, but delay brought economic consequences.

While the ship's owner and crew debated the decision, Paul brought a warning. The voyage, he predicted, would end with disaster and the loss of both cargo and the lives aboard. The Bible does not say how he knew this, though it appears to have been a spiritually-supplied insight. The centurion in charge, however, was persuaded by the owner and helmsman to attempt the forty mile trip to Phoenix, which provided better shelter for the winter. So when a gentle southerly breeze began to blow, the ship put out to sea. (Acts 27: 9-13)

The soft wind did not last long. Shortly out of port, a fierce northeast wind of hurricane force, known locally as *Euroclydon,* arose suddenly, slamming the boat off course. So ferocious a storm could propel a craft anywhere, or simply batter it until it sank. The owner and centurion had gambled and lost.

The Storm

In severe storms, ships attempt to sail directly into oncoming winds. Otherwise, waves will strike the sides of a boat, potentially shattering or capsizing the vessel. When the alarmed sailors saw they could not head into the wind, they used a back-up strategy. The sails were lowered, allowing the wind to drive the boat wherever it wished. At the same time, sturdy rope was wrapped around the ship's hull for greater structural strength. Finally, the small skiff that doubled as a lifeboat, which was usually towed, was pulled aboard and secured. This was probably done to prevent it from repeatedly crashing into the ship, which would have damaged or destroyed both craft. (Acts 27: 14-17)

The storm grew worse, and so further and more desperate steps were taken. First cargo was thrown overboard, followed by the ship's tackle. Lightening the boat was essential to survival; everything that could be spared was flung into the tumultuous sea—and still the storm raged. Darkness shrouded them for days, blotting both sun and stars and darkening the hopes of all aboard. It was impossible to navigate or even know where the wind was driving them; perhaps it was toward rocky shoals where disaster would strike without warning. Hope faded day by day, replaced by the grim belief they would probably perish in the storm.

Just when things were at their darkest, Paul stood in their midst and spoke the first words of hope heard since the storm's onset. First, he threw in a little "I told you so"—probably not so much to rub it in as to encourage the centurion to heed his advice in the future. Then came the cheering words welcomed by all. An angel of the living God had stood by his side and told him he would keep his appointment with Caesar. For good measure,

God had graciously given him the lives of all else on the ship; not a one would be lost. The voyage would end, he foresaw, by running aground on a nearby island. (Acts 27: 21-25)

Shortly after Paul's encouraging words, the crew could tell through soundings[4] they were finally near land. Grounding a boat, however, was hazardous under the best of conditions. A few sailors decided their chances were better if they could secretly escape in the skiff. They lowered the small boat in the water on a pretense that Paul saw through immediately. His words to the centurion were brief and chilling: *"Unless these men stay in the ship, you cannot be saved."* The centurion had learned his lesson about Paul's advice. Immediately, the ropes were hacked and the skiff drifted away unmanned. (Acts 27: 30-32)

Tension still ran high among the 276 occupants of the battered ship. People were weak from stress, lack of food and probably from a lack of sleep. (Through anxiety, seasickness or both, the people had stopped eating). Gradually the boat drew closer to land and Paul encouraged everyone to take some food—they would need strength for the coming trial of leaving the boat. As people obeyed and gathered to eat, Paul took bread and gave thanks to God. It was an act communion—eating as the early Christians ate—and its effect was immediate: *"Then they were all encouraged."* (Acts 27:36)

Getting Out of the Boat

Daylight revealed an island they did not recognize, and the even more welcome sight of a beach. Here before them was the slim chance to get ashore, away from the murderous fury of the sea; to walk on land again and live to tell the story of those terrifying weeks. Cautiously, they struck the sails and glided toward the ribbon-thin beach on the horizon. Their soaring hopes were jarred abruptly when the boat caught on a sandbar, the beach before them a short but dangerous swim away.

Waves furiously pounded the rear of the ship, as if the sea was angry over its escaping prey. The vessel would be destroyed—there was no question of that—and so orders were given for all to abandon ship. In these circumstances, the standard procedure for soldiers of that time was to kill all prisoners. Roman military law dictated that a soldier who allowed a prisoner to escape forfeited his own life in exchange. The centurion, however, was determined to save the life of this extraordinary prisoner named Paul. Instead, orders were given for all to get ashore. Those who could swim jumped in the water, flailing against the undertow of receding waves that threatened to drag them back to sea. Others, too fatigued or unable to swim, clung to pieces of the ship and struggled toward the shore. Hours later, the exhausted passengers and crew staggered or crawled onto the beach. As they took account of those present, the centurion made a remarkable discovery; just as Paul had said, everyone was alive. God had, indeed, graciously given the apostle the lives of all who traveled with him.

Lessons From Leaving the Boat

The movie character Forrest Gump had a way to describe the unexpected twists and turns of life. His mother had told him: "Life is like a box of chocolates. You never know what you're gonna get." People make plans, but God has purposes. There's quite a difference between the two: our plans can't help but come from our limited perspective. We catch a glimpse of a small scene, but God sees the whole panorama of time at once. This is why He can be said to have *purposes*. Just the same, disrupted plans are rarely pleasant. The process of growing in faith does not come from picking over the ruins of our plans and asking *why?* It comes from asking the only right and sensible question for a servant; *what do you wish me to do in the detour you have brought?*

It is a new type of thinking that is easier said than done. The decision to trust and look for God's purposes—*particularly* through struggles—becomes the process that transforms us into the image of Christ, and grows us into children of God. God is making us into wonderful eternal beings that look like Him—the kind of being which, if we saw now, we might be tempted to worship. But the process of transformation comes through unmaking what we are now and recreating, even metamorphosing, with all the pain and messiness of that process.

Any plans we make that do not match His wonderful purposes must be undone; there is simply no other possible way. Our whole perspective, especially our view of disrupted plans, must be unmade. Simply put, God disrupts our plans for our own good. We see this process continually in life. It is the coach or tutor who demands our time and makes us work toward excellence. It is the doctor who understands our symptoms when we do not, and disrupts our plans by admitting us to the hospital. What we think of as *disruptions* may actually be getting back on course.

Getting a New Perspective

Let's look briefly at how Paul and a group of passengers bound for Rome had a change of perspective. First, they left their battered craft with gratitude and thanksgiving. They did not expect to live, and getting to land was like a last-minute reprieve from a death sentence. Developing an attitude of gratitude requires a conscious decision—a willingness to say that God is in control of all things. Paul had just such an attitude in his preparation to leave the boat. Just before his boat ground into the sandbar, he assembled everyone for a meal and needed words of encouragement. What did he do first? The account says he gave thanks. (Acts 27:35)

Perspective shapes our views whether we see it operating or not. As one wag observed, impending death has a way of wonderfully focusing the mind. The job we disliked may not seem so bad when unemployment drags out longer than we thought. Perspective forces us to deal with reality, and not an idealized scene that no longer exists. It recognizes our past and what God has done, and often the place from which He has brought us. At the same time, thanksgiving does not live in the past. It does not dwell on what was lost, but sees provision and kindness in the present.

Try to imagine yourself in that boat with Paul. In the worst of the storm, would you have traded all your goods on the boat to stand safely on shore? Obviously you would. Paul's gratitude was a matter of perspective. It's tempting to see this as nothing more than a optimist's "half full" glass of water—but that would be a mistake. A perspective of thanksgiving is nothing more than a correct view of God, and seeing our lives in the grand design of his plans. The first step in leaving the boat of disrupted plans is to tune our hearts to God's melody in an attitude of thanksgiving.

Second, Paul left the boat encouraging others. Even before the boat ran aground, Paul exhorted everyone present to take heart and eat some food. He reminded them that "not a single hair" would fall from anyone's head; this powerfully invoked

Jesus' teaching about God's care for us. *"Are not two sparrows sold for a penny? Yet, not one of them falls to the ground apart from your Father's will. But the very hairs of your head are all numbered. Do not fear therefore; you are of more value than many sparrows."* (Matthew 10: 29-31, NKJV) The psalmist, King David, noted that God's thoughts about us are more numerous than the number of grains of sand on the beach. (Psalm 139: 17-18) God's care for us and attention to the circumstances of our lives is beyond human calculation. Out of the richness of his own relationship with God, Paul reminded others of God's character. The idea of encouragement is to urge forward, or persuade. This is how God would have us lead others with whom we find ourselves in disrupted plans.

Third, Paul left the boat of disrupted plans with confidence that God's plans cannot be thwarted. His strength came from beyond the storm, secretly nourished by God's kindness and the conviction God's plans will prevail. What God allows is simply His means of getting us where we need to be. Even the acts of others intended for evil can be turned to God's purposes. Joseph, the son of Jacob, was sold into slavery by his brothers, but later told them ""(Y)ou meant evil against me; but God meant it for good…" (Gen 50: 20 NKJV) Getting out of a boat of disrupted plans is all about regaining a right perspective.

Mike's Story

My old friend Mike is a remarkable man. Born in a tough neighborhood in the Bronx in New York City, he grew up on the streets and learned how to survive. He was a Golden Gloves boxer who thought he had to fight everyone to get by. Mike ended up joining the New York City Police Department, but remained the angry tough guy from the street, always ready to fight.

Things changed for Mike one winter night when he wandered past a small storefront church. He could hear singing inside, and the joyous sounds gripped him. How could people be so happy in life? Mike remembers feeling irresistibly drawn into that small church, where he sat in the back and heard the gospel. The anger and old ways melted away and Mike experienced a remarkable conversion to faith in Jesus Christ. He went to all his friends and announced proudly that he was now "born again."

Shortly after that wonderful night, on a bitterly cold Christmas Eve, Mike walked through a night of disrupted plans that could have been disastrous. While alone on his beat in Harlem, a call came from a terrified subway token clerk. The trains had stopped running on an elevated train station on Mike's beat, and the scene had turned ugly quickly. It was 4 degrees below zero; a switch further down the line was frozen, and trains could not advance beyond that point. Furious patrons pounded on the windows at the booth, screaming and venting their fury while the petrified clerk pleaded to no avail. Mike quickly mounted the stairs and came face to face with the angry mob. The crowd turned its attention from the booth and began encircling him, threats erupting here and next there.

Mike prayed a quick and silent prayer and then addressed the crowd. He knew a single officer was no match for a mob, and needed all his wits. As he pleaded for calm, Mike addressed the crowd to say he was calling for a coffee vendor he had passed on the street below. Tonight, he announced, the City of New York was buying hot beverages for everyone. The happy vendor rushed to bring coffee and hot chocolate to eager hands, which grasped cups as quickly as they arrived. Then Mike addressed the crowd again and said "Look, most of you here are Christians and it's Christmas Eve. Let's move over by the heaters on the wall and sing Christmas carols together." Surprised faces exchanged looks throughout the crowd, and everyone started shuffling over toward the small heaters. Then Mike raised his nightstick like a conductor and his raspy voice began singing *Silent night ... holy night ... all is calm...* No one was more surprised than Mike when voices everywhere joined him. It was like a dream; the entire platform filled with voices singing Silent Night, and then voices below on the street began joining in. Music filled the block and kept spreading—voices singing a capella around them, spreading into the frigid Harlem night. As far as the ear could ear, the night was filled with singing.

The singing continued for a while, but no one watched the time that miraculous evening. Suddenly lights surged on at the platform and a dead train came to life and rolled up to the passengers. Mike walked over to the open doors of the nearest car, immediately refreshed by the blast of heat from within. Then, the passengers lined up to thank Mike before boarding the train. Men gave him high fives, and a few women even kissed him on the cheek. One very large man looked down on him with a smile and said "You're alright, man." It was an experience Mike would never forget. When Mike's replacement arrived hours later, Mike said to him "You won't believe what happened tonight; it was a miracle!" The replacement, knowing Mike's unorthodox reputation, replied "I'd rather not hear." Yet, the replacement looked around and admitted he felt something in the air; somehow, magically, the afterglow of *Silent Night* still lingered. Perhaps angels, unseen, had joined the choir that evening.

But Mike's story gets more interesting. Years later, Mike retired from the force and went into full time ministry. He had the ability to touch hearts and reach all kinds of people in different cultures. From his police days, Mike understood the unique pressures on police officers and their families, and began a special ministry to them. God blessed his work, first in New York City, then throughout the United States, and finally throughout the world. He has been invited to numerous police departments where he shares his story and founds chapters of Christian police officers.

Mike comes to mind as well because of a unique connection to the story of Paul's shipwreck. During one of his trips, as Mike ministered throughout Italy, an invitation came to the meet with police and afterward speak in a church in Siracusa (or Syracuse) in Sicily. The adventurous Mike was happy to accept. Unknown to him, the local church had a long-standing tradition that Saint Paul himself had been its founder. Mike turned in his Bible to the account of Paul's disrupted voyage and discovered that after the unplanned stop in Malta, Paul had traveled to Syracuse and stayed three days while on his trip to Rome. (Acts 28:12) In the church that evening he read the account of Paul's shipwreck. "Look!" he exclaimed to them, "The Apostle Paul was here on your island!— do you realize what you had?"

The effect of the little account was remarkable on the crowd. Eager ears wanted to hear more from the American who had been a police officer in New York City. As Mike told me the story, and how God moved that night, I could only wonder at God's providence. Here, so many centuries later, he was still using Paul's disrupted journey for his purposes. Isn't that just like God?

CHAPTER SEVEN: A BOAT CALLED DOUBT

"Only God and the sea know where the great ship has gone…"
Woodrow Wilson

The Cyclops

One of the strangest mysteries of maritime history is the fate of the USS Cyclops. The ship and its 306 crew and passengers vanished in 1918, though to this day the circumstances remain a mystery. Its disappearance remains the largest non-combat loss of life in US Naval history. Dr. Clive Cussler of the National Underwater and Marine Agency noted "(t)he Cyclops still remains the largest navy ship ever lost without leaving the slightest clue to her fate.

The *Cyclops* was large for her time; built in 1910, the 19,360 ton ship was built to haul coal and supply fuel for mobile battle fleets. With the outbreak of WW I, the *Cyclops* was commissioned on May 1, 1917. According to naval records, she served in various war efforts and in early 1918 sailed for Brazil to fuel British ships in the south Atlantic. Her last known voyage started when she put to sea from Rio de Janeiro on February 16, 1918. She stopped briefly in the Brazilian City of Bahia and then departed for Baltimore, Maryland, carrying over 10,000 tons of ore. Her last known contact was an unscheduled stop in Barbados on March 3rd, where she took on extra supplies. The *Cyclops* pushed out to sea again, scheduled to arrive in Baltimore around March 13th. She would never arrive at her destination, vanishing without a trace or any clue to her fate.

Speculations

The mysterious disappearance has fueled rumors ranging from the predictable to the supernatural. Most credible speculations focus on storms, though equipment failure may have been a contributing factor. According to contemporary records, the starboard engine had a cracked cylinder and was scheduled for repair in the U.S. There are also claims that the ship was overloaded when she left Brazil, which would have made her more prone to capsizing in bad weather.

Other speculation concerns the boat's captain, George W. Worley. Worley, who was born in Hanover, Germany, had changed his name from Johan Frederick Wichmann after arriving in the United States. There were persistent reports that Worley was a German sympathizer. One telegram, received by the Secretary of State after *Cyclops'* disappearance, noted that "many Germanic names" appeared in the crew and passenger list.

More interestingly, it was said Worley was a brutal man with a Captain Bligh (of HMS Bounty fame) type personality. Stories abounded of his harsh discipline over minor infractions, and even an execution. On one occasion he reportedly chased an ensign around the ship with a pistol. There are also accounts that raise questions about Worley's sanity. As one example, reports claimed he would make rounds on the ship wearing long underwear and a derby hat.

There is ample evidence showing that Worley was despised by his crew. This has led to speculation on whether the crew mutinied and went into hiding after disposing of Worley, but there is not a shred of evidence to support this. It's hard to imagine how a boat and crew, to say nothing of a mutiny, could be hidden for almost a century.

Fans of the *Bermuda Triangle* theory also point to *Cyclops'* disappearance as proof of whatever mysterious force they believe to be at work in that region. *Triangle* enthusiasts note that no distress signal was given by the ship, though with the primitive communications of that day, a ship that overturned would likely not have had time to send an SOS. Befitting its mysterious disappearance, the *Cyclops* figures prominently in several books and the Sci Fi Channel's special on *"The Triangle."* It even rated a mention in an episode of the animated cartoon *Scooby Do* set in the Bermuda Triangle.

Mysteries appeal to some instinct in human nature, and unsolved mysteries are particularly intriguing. Uncertainty is the root of doubt, though not all doubt is bad. There is a doubt that leads to prudent questions, or that expresses skepticism over claims that sound too good to be true. Doubt may be a form of prudence, but at other times doubt—or uncertainty—wars against faith. Why is this so critical? Because the Bible asserts that *without faith it is impossible to please God.* Biblical faith believes that God exists, and that He rewards those who diligently seek Him. (Hebrews 11:6) Since doubt can be either prudent or faithless, how do we determine which form is at work in our lives? There may be times that doubt takes us to crossroads, where one way leads towards a lack of faith. Let's look at a story of doubt at that critical juncture, and what goes into a decision to route doubt into faith.

A Wasted Night's Work

Peter's muscular arms yanked at the nets draped over the side of his boat. Sighing gently he noted the weight; the nets offered little resistance, which meant they were nearly empty. He and his partners had toiled all night with nothing to show for it. Still, there was always one reward for a fisherman, no matter how bad the catch: sunrise on the Sea of Galilee. Rose and gold tinged fingers of light crept from behind the hills to the east, reflecting flecks on the surface, turning the water red, then gold and then pale yellow. He could spare a few minutes to enjoy the sight; then it was time to return home and clean the nets.

The town would be coming to life, with vendors in the market laying out wares and women and children working at the lake's edge. Only this particular morning something was different; a large crowd was assembled by the shore—larger than any he could recall—and growing every minute. The men in the two boats exchanged questioning looks over the growing crowd. The disappointment of a bad catch was replaced by curiosity as the boats crept toward the shore. As he drew nearer, Peter caught sight of a person who was clearly the center of interest; his heart raced when he recognized the prophet and miracle worker from Nazareth.

Both boats pulled to shore, and Peter and his friends climbed out wearily dragging their gear behind them. There was still the work of mending and cleaning nets to be ready for the next effort, and from this location they could tend to work and listen to the teacher. By the time Jesus was ready to speak, the crowd was immense and unmanageable. People everywhere shoved and jostled to get as close as possible and the line of humanity inched closer to Jesus, nearly forcing him into the water. Jesus glanced at Peter's boat and suddenly walked toward Peter and climbed into the craft. The unexpected action both pleased Peter and made him nervous, but he readily obeyed when Jesus asked him to drag the boat a short distance from the shore. (This account is found, generally, in Luke 5: 1-10)

Once settled, Jesus began teaching the crowd—speaking as He always did in parables and mysterious references to His Father. After He finished teaching, Jesus dismissed the crowd and then fixed his gaze on Peter. With a faint smile He told Peter to launch his boat back into deep water and cast the nets to catch fish.

Peter wrestled inwardly with irritation and confusion; this was crazy talk. Coming from anyone else he would have given the speaker an earful of a fisherman's choicest words of frustration. This, however, was different. With Jesus in the picture, Peter had already learned the usual rules did not apply. Still, doubt clouded his mind. Jesus was a gifted rabbi with astonishing authority, but not a fisherman. What could a carpenter turned rabbi possibly know about fishing? This command was a foolish waste of time, and Peter was exhausted from the night's labors. The decision hung before him for a moment—doubt versus the desire to trust this man, and the latter won out. With a skeptical shrug, Peter replied in a way that would forever change his life: "Master, we worked hard all night and caught nothing; but because you are telling me to do this I'll drop the nets." He found himself mouthing the words, though in truth he felt only a slight glimmer of expectation.

For I am a Sinful Man

Peter's small boat drifted out into deeper water. Mechanically, as he had done dozens of times the night before, he flung the nets out onto the now still surface. The ropes hit with a loud slap and the weighted nets drifted slowly below the surface. Minutes ticked by, and Peter tugged the ropes mechanically, more out of habit than expectation. As his gnarly hands pulled there was an unexpected sensation; there was resistance—lots of it—as if a great weight rested in the ropes. He yanked again and again, and still it was the same. His friends in the boat gathered next to him and they pulled together. It was still too heavy, even for all of them. *What was in this net?*

Peter called to James and John in the other craft and they hurried to his side. Now hands from both boats grasped the net and pulled. It rose slowly, revealing a silvery mass of wiggling and jumping fish. It was astonishing. The men started bailing fish into their boats to lighten the nets, only it seemed the stream of fish was unending. The nets, repaired only hours before, popped and tore under the strain. Even more remarkably, both boats were in danger of sinking from the weight.

Peter turned to the figure of Jesus, seated silently in the boat, with mingled amazement and fear. This was impossible; *who was this man?* It must be the presence of God at work, once again, through this extraordinary Rabbi. There seemed only one possible response for Peter. He dropped to his knees, head bowed, and said: "Go away from me Lord, for I am a sinful man." (Luke 5:8)

It's easy to understand Peter's reaction. Suddenly confronted by the presence of God, our spiritual eyes instinctively turn inward—and what we see is not pretty. Our failures and hypocrisies come readily to mind, accusing and reminding us of our "real" selves. The mind in this state wants to escape from God—to create greater distance from the holy source of our distress. This was exactly Peter's reaction: put distance between us quickly, because you don't get how bad I am.

Jesus' reply immediately put Peter at peace: "Do not be afraid; from now on you will be catching men (instead of fish)." That was good enough for Peter. The men dragged their boats to the shore and emptied the catch, and then did something more remarkable. They walked away from their livelihood and followed Jesus, wherever that road would lead.

A Boat Called Doubt

In that moment when Peter dropped to his knees to say "Depart from me...," what reply do you think he *expected?* What reply do you think he *wished* to hear? Was it the same as what he expected? I suspect not. My guess is that Peter expected rejection because of his many imperfections. We doubt our usefulness to God because we see those imperfections. It is difficult to accept that we have value to God in our fallen state. It was not false humility that drove an apprehensive Peter to his knees.

What reply did Peter wish to hear? I suspect his best hope was something like this: *Yes, you are a sinful man and a mess as well. Still, I can probably find something for you to do after we work you over and you learn to behave better.* Instead, he heard an answer that surpassed his expectations. Essentially, Jesus invited him to "follow"—to devote his life and efforts as a disciple—*just as he was.* More than that, Jesus did not focus on what Peter was at present; He looked instead to what Peter would become. He lured Peter to his destiny.

How did Jesus get Peter out of a boat called *Doubt?* Let's look at the process. Before getting to the business at hand, Jesus asked Peter for a favor. Peter had something Jesus wanted to use: a boat. Here is a fascinating truth; the God who created the universe constantly asks for little possessions which He has entrusted to us. He had need of Peter's humble little boat. On another day, Jesus miraculously fed over 5,000 people—but first, he needed a few small loaves of bread and fish from a little boy. When He would ride into Jerusalem in his triumphal entry foretold by the prophets, he first had to borrow a donkey from an unnamed man. On the occasion of the Last Supper, He needed a room to meet with His friends. Before we leave a boat of doubt, Jesus may call us to surrender or lend him some ordinary possession for his extraordinary purposes. It is a small step, but a critical one. If we will not give a seemingly small thing in obedience, He may not ask us for more. He was very clear on this point: *the one who is faithful in small things can be trusted with more.* (Matthew 25:21) To leave a Boat of Doubt we must willingly offer what we possess to God. Furthermore, we must believe that He may use our small token in a profound and even miraculous way.

The next step in leaving the boat came when Jesus met the expressed need of Peter. What was that need? Fish. He had fished all night and caught nothing. This was Peter's livelihood, but also a felt need for a man whose identity was wrapped up in his profession. Does God intend to meet our earthly needs? Absolutely! It is part of his care and providence. It sends a message we are valued and loved, even if we are not deserving of His blessing. Having said this, it is important to note God promises to meet our *needs,* and not our *greeds.* The Bible's definition of actual *needs* is a short list: food, clothing and shelter. Jesus made the point in describing God's faithfulness: the lilies of the field were beautifully dressed, and the birds of the air do not lack food. *We are of much more importance to our Father than these, and how much more will our Heavenly Father provide for us?* (Matthew 6:25-34)

In an increasingly complex society, more things feel like "needs" all the time. For example, it's hard to imagine the internet or e-mail as options and not needs; yet, by biblical standards they are not essentials of life. Whether God has officially expanded the list of "needs" makes an interesting theological debate, but that would miss the point: *God provides for our needs, and in doing so demonstrates his loving care for us.* To leave a Boat of Doubt we must be willing to offer what we have, but also to believe God will care for us as we trust Him and surrender those small possessions.

Finally, Jesus affirmed Peter's preparation and fitness for the task in a way Peter could understand. Peter was a fisherman; it was the life and skill-set he knew. He would continue fishing—except it would be for people. In the course of his new call as a "fisher of men," lessons from his strenuous life at sea undoubtedly stayed with him. Whatever we are in life, whatever we *do,* gives us a framework for God's Spirit to communicate truth. Farmers have a profound understanding of harvest and the dangers of delay; artists viscerally feel and communicate God's glorious creation; my own profession (a lawyer) gives me a profound appreciation for the legal-type transaction that brought our salvation. What you do impacts the way God's truth is perceived, and in turn gives you a unique way to communicate truth to others.

God wants to work in our lives through whatever talents and

abilities He has given. Are you a carpenter? You may be called to build for His kingdom. Perhaps you are a teacher or laborer; you may be called to teach about His glory, or labor for His will to be accomplished. A doctor? He may call you to be a healer of people for His glory. He simply asks us to believe the call, and accept the value He sees in us.

The Danger of Doubt

It is important to remember that doubt is not always bad. Doubt may be the beginning of an honest examination of something that does not make sense, or the natural skepticism we feel for something that does not ring true. Theologian Paul Tillich once noted *"Doubt isn't the opposite of faith; it is an element of faith."* How true! Faith by its very nature requires doubt, for nothing less than the struggle with uncertainty can bring the triumph of overcoming faith. There is no option: doubt will move us along the path of faith, but we determine its direction—either closer to or farther from God.

While doubt may be an element of faith, there is also the danger it will grow into unbelief. Doubt is merely the uncertainty we feel when a decision lies before us. When we resolve doubt against trusting God and His promises, it begins its terrible transformation into faithlessness. Persistent and willful unbelief ultimately separates us from God. Consider the words of the author of Hebrews: *"And to whom did He swear that that they would not enter into His rest, but to those who did not obey? So we see they could not enter in because of unbelief. Beware, brethren, lest there be in any of you an evil heart of unbelief in departing from the living God."* (Hebrews 3: 18-19, 12 NKJV) For good reason, the Bible warns that without faith it is *impossible* to please God.

What causes doubt to transform into unbelief? Often it is self-interest. Doubt clouds our minds when we worry about how a decision will affect us. It weighs the effect of a choice on considerations like our finances, safety, or how people will view us. God's interests, on the other hand, always lie with others. Peter was not called to be a fisherman to increase his material wealth, but to catch and save the lives of others separated from God. He and John would later say "Silver and gold we do not have, *but what we do have we give to you.* In the name of Jesus Christ of Nazareth, rise up and walk." (Acts 3:6) Peter lost the material rewards of his fishing career for an eternal and magnificent treasure. He lost the approval of political and religious leaders to become a friend of God. And finally, he would lose his very life as a martyr to gain eternal life in glory.

When we are consumed with our personal welfare, we lose our vision of God; we no longer care as much about neighbors or friends. Our time of communion with God in prayer and worship is replaced by worry over finances. Our desire for fellowship is squeezed out by distractions and time demands that cry out with increasing urgency. If we are honest with ourselves, we can all recognize times when these symptoms appear. It may be that doubt is at the root. Doubt in a series of small decisions builds slowly to unbelief; but it is never too late with God for a willing heart. Resolve it for yourself even now; get out of the boat called doubt and follow the call of Jesus.

Dietrich Bonhoeffer

The date was April 9, 1945, less than a month before the end of WW II. While cannons boomed in the background and allied forces pressed closer to the scene, seven bedraggled prisoners in the German extermination camp of Flossenburg huddled together awaiting their execution. One of the seven was the German theologian, Dietrich Bonhoeffer. Bonhoeffer had been implicated in the failed plot to kill Adolph Hitler the year before, and would now suffer the terrible fate of enemies of the Reich: he would be hanged naked by piano wire and suffer a slow and excruciatingly painful death. Bonhoeffer was only 39 years old, but in his short life produced an extraordinary legacy.

Born in Breslau in 1906, Dietrich was his family's fourth son and sixth child. His father, Karl Bonhoeffer, was a famous psychiatrist and professor at a prestigious university. Young Dietrich showed exceptional talent for playing the piano and seemed destined for a career in music. To the surprise of his family, at the age of 14 he announced that instead of studying music, he planned to become a minister and theologian. Not everyone in the family was enthusiastic about his decision.

Bonhoeffer excelled academically, first at Tubingen University for a year and then at the University of Berlin. He completed his dissertation on *The Communion of Saints* at the age of 21; a leading theologian of the day later acknowledged his thesis as a "theological miracle." After taking a teaching position at the university, he accepted a fellowship at Union Theological Seminary in New York. His experiences in the U.S. affected him profoundly. On his return to NY, friends and students noticed the change. When pressed on what had happened to him abroad, he replied simply that he had become a Christian.

Bonhoeffer became a popular lecturer and developed a reputation as one unafraid to question the status quo of religious-academic traditions. He challenged his students to search for authentic expressions of Christianity, even as he made time in his busy schedule to minister in the slums of Berlin. He continued to grow in stature, while a malignant shadow drew over Germany.

The 1930s would bring the ascendancy of Adolph Hitler and National Socialism, better known today as Nazism. In time, the Nazis would demand unflinching loyalty from the churches throughout the Reich. Sadly, many pastors publicly aligned with the Nazis, and eventually signed pledges that they would not criticize the government or its policies. The failure to cooperate brought increasingly severe consequences. In time, Bonhoeffer would be caught and progressively squeezed in the Nazi vise.

Bonhoeffer did not limit his activities to public opposition to Hitler, and encouraged other Christians to vote against National Socialism candidates. He also pleaded with the Church to remain independent from the Nazi Party and its ideals, but found himself increasingly a voice in the wilderness. In 1934, Bonhoeffer and other pastors formed the so-called "Confessing Church," which opposed Nazi policies. The group equated the Nazi pledge for churches with idolatry, making the signers marked men with the Gestapo. Their founding confession boldly proclaimed: *"We repudiate the false teaching that there are areas of our life in which we belong not to Jesus Christ but to other lords.... "*

Unsurprisingly, Bonhoeffer was denied a pastorate a few years later. By that time, ordination required proof of both pure German lineage *and* loyalty to Nazism. Adding to his growing list of tensions with the Nazis was the government's increasing persecution of Jews in Germany. Bonhoeffer was one of the most vocal and valiant opponents of the virulent anti-Semitism spreading throughout Germany, which furthered the ire of the Gestapo.

Bonhoeffer continued his opposition to the Nazis and their policies over the next few years, but was frustrated by the absence of outrage in the German Church; even his friends in the "Confessing Church" did not go as far in their opposition as he wished.

Eventually, it was apparent to Bonhoeffer and his friends that war was inevitable. Worse yet, he certainly would be called to serve in the military. That call of service would have required taking an oath of loyalty to *the Fuehrer*, which he could not do. In a highly nationalistic environment, his failure to do so would bring shame upon him and his friends, even among other Christians. There seemed to be no good alternative but leaving his beloved homeland. Fighting discouragement, Bonhoeffer left Germany in 1939 and moved to America at the invitation of Union Theological Seminary. It was during this stay in New York that he reached what was arguably the most fateful decision of his life in ministry.

The Return to Germany

Bonhoeffer would remain in the safety of America for only four weeks. The decision to leave Germany was agonizing for him, even with the knowledge of his peril. His diary during this period is filled with anxiety and regret over leaving Germany during her hour of peril. While praying for inspiration during his brief stay he came upon a verse in Isaiah: *He who believes does not flee.* (Probably a reference to Isa. 28:16) There was no other possible outcome for him from that time forward; he would return to Germany regardless of his almost certain fate. He booked passage on the last steamship to cross the Atlantic for years.

The picture of Bonhoeffer boarding that boat sailing into the jaws of hell staggers the imagination. In a modern age so self-absorbed and preoccupied with comfort, such courage is nearly inconceivable. Just before his departure, Bonhoeffer wrote to his friend Reinhold Niebuhr with this explanation:

"I have come to the conclusion that I made a mistake in coming to America. I must live through this difficult period in our national history with

the people of Germany. I will have no right to participate in the reconstruction of Christian life in Germany after the war if I do not share the trials of this time with my people... Christians in Germany will have to face the terrible alternative of either willing the defeat of their nation in order that Christian civilization may survive or willing the victory of their nation and thereby destroying civilization. I know which of these alternatives I must choose but I cannot make that choice from security."

Once back in Germany, Bonhoeffer was forbidden to preach, and even to speak or write publicly without government approval. The Gestapo monitored all his activities, and required him to report regularly. Despite all this scrutiny, he was able to connect with and eventually join the plotters intending to kill Hitler. Bonhoeffer's lectures on discipleship during this time would later be gathered and published in the classic for which he is best remembered today, *The Cost of Discipleship*. Throughout the book he warns of the danger of *cheap grace*, or faith that costs us nothing. Bonhoeffer wrote, but more importantly, modeled this warning—even at the very cost of his life.

On April 5, 1943 the inevitable arrest came. Initially, the Nazis lacked specifics, but were able to connect Bonhoeffer's activities to a plan to rescue Jews in Germany. While in prison, he continued to write letters and poems that are among his most inspiring surviving works. In the course of time following the unsuccessful attempt on Hitler's life in 1944, his name would be drawn into the ever-widening net of conspirators. Mere suspicion of complicity was sufficient to bring the prescribed dreadful method of execution.

The little we know of Bonhoeffer's last days comes from the book *The Venlo Incident*, written by a fellow prisoner, British Officer Payne Best. Best would later say: "He was one of the very few men I have ever met to whom his God was real and ever close to him..." The final known words of his life were spoken to Best the day the executioners came to their shared cell: "This is the end—for me, the beginning of life." The brutal execution—the beginning of true life—was carried out on April 9, 1945. A camp doctor assigned to witness executions watched as Bonhoeffer knelt and prayed. He described the execution this way: "I was most deeply moved by the way this lovable man prayed, so devout and so certain that God heard his prayer..." At the place of execution, he again said a short prayer and then climbed the steps to the gallows, brave and composed.... In the almost fifty years that I worked as a doctor, I have hardly ever seen a man die so entirely submissive to the will of God."

Doubt

While this extraordinary story still inspires us, why is it included in a chapter about *Doubt*? As I studied Bonhoeffer's life and writings, I was struck with the question whether he had wrestled with doubt in some way. Every detail of Bonhoeffer's life, down to the leaving of it, seemed marked by certainty and conviction. I found myself wondering *did he ever wrestle with doubts about his sufficiency to walk so difficult a course?* I think one of the last poems written before his death sheds some interesting light on this question. Reproduced below is Bonhoeffer's beloved poem, *Who Am I*. The italics are added.

WHO AM I?

Who am I? They often tell me
I would step from my cell's confinement
Calmly, cheerfully, firmly,
Like a squire from his country-house.
Who am I? They often tell me
I would talk to my warders
freely and friendly and clearly,
as though it were mine to command.
Who am I? They also tell me
I would bear the days of misfortune
Equably, smilingly, proudly,
Like one accustomed to win.
Am I then really all that which men tell of?
Or am I only what I know of myself,
Restless and longing and sick like a bird in a cage,
Struggling for breath, as though hands were compressing my throat,
Yearning for colours, for flowers, for the voices of birds,
Thirsting for words of kindness, for neighborliness,
Trembling with anger at despotisms and petty humiliation,
Tossing in expectation of great events,
Powerlessly trembling for friends at an infinite distance,
Weary and empty at praying, at thinking, at making
Faint, and ready to say farewell to it all?
Who am I? This or the other?
Am I one person today, and tomorrow another?
Am I both at once? A hypocrite before others,
And before myself a contemptibly woebegone weakling?
Or is something within me still like a beaten army,
Fleeing in disorder from victory already achieved?
Who am I? They mock me, these lonely questions of mine.
Whoever I am, thou knowest, O God, I am thine.

138

The eloquent expression of Bonhoeffer's doubt speaks for itself. Here is the beautiful paradox of hope, and of faith, and of God's ultimately prevailing grace. We need not let doubt cripple us or keep us from God's great purposes. His grace is sufficient to bring us through doubt to faith.

Bonhoeffer doubted his sufficiency for the terrible fate that faced him back in Germany. Yet, he was willing to accept that God would be sufficient for the task at hand. Many centuries before, the Apostle Peter accepted a similar call to follow Jesus. He did so, even though the resurrected Jesus foretold that Peter would also suffer the fate of crucifixion under the cruel Roman regime. (John 21: 18-19) According to tradition, when the time of Peter's death arrived, he asked to be crucified upside-down, being unworthy to die in the same manner as his Lord. The Romans obliged his request.

Knowing all this, Peter and Bonhoeffer shared the perspective of a call to suffering and even death. With the knowledge of what was coming, Peter would pen the words that have inspired and touched so many Christians in times of suffering: "Beloved, do not think it strange concerning the fiery trial which is come to try you, as though some strange thing happened to you; but rejoice to the extent that you partake of Christ's sufferings, that when His glory is revealed, you may also be glad with exceeding joy."
(1 Peter 4:12, NKJV) Perhaps Bonhoeffer himself was inspired by those words.

Doubt in our ability to follow the Lord's calling is the common experience of Christians. Someone once noted that courage is not the absence of fear, but rather the willingness to proceed in the face of fear. Perhaps a similar thing could be said about faith; biblical faith is not the absence of doubt, but the willingness to follow Christ and obey in doubt.

CHAPTER EIGHT: A BOAT CALLED DELIVERANCE

A miracle of deliverance, achieved by valor, by perseverance, by perfect discipline, by faultless service, by resource, by skill, by unconquerable fidelity, is manifest to us all.
Winston Churchill on the Dunkirk evacuation

The Dunkirk Evacuation

As we have seen, there are many boats in life best avoided; but the opposite is also true. There are times that rescue comes from *getting in* rather than out of a boat. This final chapter is about boats that save rather than harm. It is the story of a boat—or rather a fleet of boats—called Deliverance.

A Disaster in the Making

The spring of 1940 was a terrible time for Western Europe. A new style of warfare, *blitzkrieg, or "lightning war,"* shocked the world, as the Nazi war machine rolled ruthlessly over nation after nation. In May of 1940 alone, German troops smashed through the Low Countries, Belgium, Luxembourg and the Netherlands, and stormed into France by circling north of the *Maginot Line*— the French defense on the German border.

Shocked British, Canadian and French troops struggled in vain against the onslaught, retreating in steps to a pocket around the harbor Dunkirk on the French coast. To all concerned, the situation looked like certain disaster for the allied forces. In desperation, the British instituted a rescue plan, code-named *Dynamo*, to evacuate as many troops as possible back to England. Privately, the British thought they would be lucky to rescue 50,000 men. Prime Minister Winston Churchill prepared the English House of Commons for the coming "colossal military disaster." The blow to England if these troops were lost was nearly incalculable. In Churchill's words, "(T)he whole root and core and brain of the British Army" was stranded on these beaches.

Then, in a fateful decision, Hitler ordered his tanks to cease pursuit of the fleeing allied troops. The reasons for this are still debated, though some suggest he was concerned the tanks would be bogged down in the rivers and canals around Dunkirk. For whatever reason, the German ground pursuit ceased, giving a new lease to the allied soldiers. Hitler considered the possibility of an evacuation, but was assured by his commanders that the *Luftwaffe*, the German Airforce, could prevent an effective escape.

The Evacuation

On May 26 the evacuation began in earnest, though there was not much optimism that any effective scale rescue could be accomplished. On the first day, 7,001 men were evacuated. Meanwhile, the British hastily assembled a fleet of 850 boats. Of this fleet, 700 boats comprised the famous "little ships of Dunkirk;" an astonishing armada of small pleasure and fishing boats, sloops, ferries, merchant marine craft, barges and nearly anything else that could float and carry troops. These small craft ferried soldiers to the larger British destroyers in deeper waters, and in some cases made the dangerous voyage with soldiers back to Dover, only to turn around and return to the evacuation. Almost miraculously the stranded soldiers were evacuated in growing numbers.

During the evacuation, the German Air Force harassed the effort, strafing boats and beaches with gunfire, even as German artillery pounded the area. Ironically, rescue ships were guided to the correct area by the smoke and glowing flames from enormous plumes of fire. German planes even dropped flares to better illuminate their targets. The British countered the German Air Force with the British RAF, dueling valiantly in the skies just over the massive evacuation effort. Though there were casualties in the evacuation, the overall effort was extraordinarily successful.

Arthur D. Divine manned one of the boats in the rescue effort. His memorable account includes the following description of the rescue[1]:

It was dark before we were well clear of the English coast. It wasn't rough, but there was a little chop on, sufficient to make it very wet, and we soaked the Admiral to the skin. Soon, in the dark, the big boats began to overtake us. We were in a sort of dark traffic lane, full of strange ghosts and weird, unaccountable waves from the wash of the larger vessels. When destroyers went by, full tilt, the wash was a serious matter to us little fellows. We could only spin the wheel to try to head into the waves, hang on, and hope for the best…

Even before it was fully dark we had picked up the glow of the Dunkirk flames, and now as we drew nearer the sailing got better, for we could steer by them and see silhouetted the shapes of other ships, of boats coming home already loaded, and of low dark shadows that might be enemy motor torpedo boats.

Then aircraft started dropping parachute flares. We saw them hanging all about us in the night, like young moons. The sound of the firing and the bombing was with us always, growing steadily louder as we got nearer and nearer. The flames grew, too. From a glow they rose up to enormous plumes of fire that roared high into the everlasting pall of smoke. As we approached Dunkirk there was an air attack on the destroyers and for a little the night was brilliant with bursting bombs and the fountain sprays of tracer bullets.

The initial rescue plan called for the recovery of about 45,000 men within two days, since the British believed a German blockade would be in place shortly. At the end of two days, about 25,000 men were ferried to safety—less than the target. But the anticipated blockade never came—and the pace of evacuation grew. On May 29, 47,000 British troops were rescued, swelling the next five days to 54,000, 68,000, 64,000, 60,000, and finally 26,000 French troops on the final night of the operation. Remarkably, a total of 338,226 soldiers were carried to safety—198,229 British and 139,997 French. Virtually the entire British force was saved from almost certain destruction or surrender. In the end, only 40,000 French troops in two divisions stayed behind to buy time for the evacuation. These brave troops eventually perished or surrendered in that final desperate stand, though their heroism purchased the rescue of their comrades.

A Miracle of Deliverance

The British public did not know the severity of the peril at Dunkirk until after the evacuation. Wartime censorship was in effect, in an effort to avoid damaging the nation's morale. Consequently, the news was kept among a few individuals. Despite this, King George VI called for a week of prayer throughout the nation. British citizens thronged their churches, cathedrals and synagogues, even as the Archbishop of Canterbury led the nation in prayers for "our soldiers in dire peril in France." Churchill noted in his memoirs:" There was a short service of intercession and prayer in Westminster Abbey. The English are loathe to expose their feelings, but in my stall in the choir I could feel the pent-up, passionate emotion, and also the fear of the congregation, not of death or wounds or material loss, but of defeat and the final ruin of Britain."

May 26 was set aside as a special day of intercession for a miraculous deliverance. While details were guarded, the British citizenry knew that some grave danger faced their troops—and they responded in nationwide prayer. When the details were finally released, Churchill described the rescue as a "miracle of deliverance." Although the British army and much of the French army at Dunkirk were rescued, Churchill was circumspect. In a speech to Parliament on June 4, he noted as follows: "*We must be careful not to assign to this deliverance the attributes of a victory. Wars are not won by evacuation. But there was a victory inside this deliverance which should be noted. It was gained by the Air Force.*"

Churchill would go on to rally a nation; he rightly noted wars are not won by evacuations, but by his own well-known formula of "blood, sweat and tears." Regardless of this truism, there was no doubt that the boats of Dunkirk pulled off a minor miracle of deliverance. We can only speculate on how history would have developed if that successful evacuation had not occurred. Still, we may imagine the return of the troops lifted the spirit of a nation and sustained its will to fight on. The heroic rescue of the British armada would one day lead to the deliverance of a nation and the defeat of Nazism.

The Deliverance of a Nation

The Bible has been described as a story of deliverance. Indeed, the main theme of the New Testament is redemption, which is about deliverance from sin and death and a restored relationship with God through Jesus Christ. The picture of deliverance was central to the nation of Israel as well, and a defining narrative in its history. Jews today still celebrate the great deliverer, Moses, who was selected by God to rescue Israel from bondage in Egypt. To this day, the great celebration of the Passover commemorates that deliverance, though for Christians it is also a picture of the redemption that would come through Jesus Christ. The towering figure of Moses would have died as a baby if a Pharaoh of Egypt had his way. Although baby Moses was born under a death sentence, he was saved by a boat called *Deliverance*.

Israel in Egypt

The history of Israel's time in Egypt goes back to the biblical patriarch Jacob. Jacob was the son of Isaac, who was the son of Abraham, and the promise of God to Abraham went through this lineage. Jacob, who was also called Israel, had twelve sons who in turn became the progenitors of the twelve tribes of Israel. Jacob's young son, Joseph, was sold by his brothers into slavery and ended up in an Egyptian household. Through turns of events he rose to the position of the second highest ruler in Egypt, second only to Pharaoh himself. (The story of Joseph and his brothers is found in Genesis from chapter 37 through chapter 50).

When a famine afflicted the ancient world of Joseph's time, his family came to Egypt where food was available though Joseph's wisdom and administrative skills. Joseph and his brothers were reconciled, and Israel settled into the land of Egypt for what would be four hundred years.

The first decades were pleasant and bountiful because of Joseph's position and influence in the land of Egypt. Over time, however, Joseph died and was forgotten. A new pharaoh arose who did not remember Joseph and saw the swelling number of Israelites as a threat. (Exodus 1:8) And so, Israel's sojourn in Egypt gradually turned into slavery. The Jews were conscripted to work on building projects for various pharaohs, and their lives became increasingly miserable under their oppressive captors. Treatment of the Israelites grew increasingly harsh, and yet their numbers grew; even in misery God's protection was with them.

The situation was not lost on the Pharaohs, who grew alarmed over the growing population. And so a fearful Pharaoh came to a dreadful solution: a death sentence. All newborn Israelite males would be drowned in the Nile River. (Exodus 1:22)

The Bible does not give much detail on how the terrible death sentence was carried out. Ancient frescoes portray Egyptian soldiers dangling infants over the Nile, as graphic reminders of this time. Fearful families likely hid their newborn children, living in dread that a cry of hunger would reach the ears of their Egyptian captors. Among the untold innumerable tragedies, the scriptures tell of one particular case and a male who was miraculously saved; this is the story of Moses, the great lawgiver who spoke directly with God.

A Boat Called Deliverance

The life of Moses is an extraordinary study in contradictions. He was born in hovel, raised in a palace and then lived in a desert wasteland. He was born to a slave and became son to a princess, labored as an unknown shepherd and finally raised up to lead a nation. Moses would come to be known as "the friend of God," and the great deliverer of his people, Israel.

The Bible tells us that Moses was a beautiful baby. His mother, driven by compassion for her child, defied Pharaoh's order and hid her son. In what must have been sparse and cramped living quarters this was not an easy task. Egyptian soldiers likely patrolled the cluster of Israelite homes, looking for telltale signs of newborn boys. With something as simple as an ill-timed cry, a baby could be carried from a home to a gruesome death in the Nile. Moses' mother hid her new baby for three months. But at the end of that time, the increasing difficulties and subterfuge became too much to handle. In a desperate act of love she conceived a plan; she would construct a small boat and place it on the very river that was intended as the instrument of cruel death. (Exodus 2:1-3)

The reedy papyrus plants growing near the Nile were very versatile; the Egyptians used them for making paper, ropes, mats and even boats. The vivid green stalks reached up to twelve feet, tapering toward the top. The original name for this papyrus came from a verb meaning, literally, *to drink* because of its remarkable absorbing properties. Moses' mother patiently gathered these papyrus stalks and wove them into a small round shape. Then she covered the bottom with a mineral pitch—the slimy bitumen that cemented and waterproofed the small boat. Once finished and hardened, the small vessel was impervious to water.

With all preparation finished, the young mother took her extraordinary and heart-breaking step of faith. Probably under cover of dark, she brought the small boat and her baby to the water's edge. She waded softly into the shallow water, and then wrapped her beloved baby in cloth and laid him gently in the basket. The child lay there in the reeds, lulled quiet for a time by the rhythmic motion of the river.

Moses' mother had not placed the basket haphazardly, for she knew where Egyptian royalty came to the river to wash. As Moses' sister Miriam watched, a daughter of Pharaoh came to the river and saw the little boat bobbing in the reeds. At her command, a maid waded to the boat and brought it to her mistress. When the royal princess unwrapped the bundle she saw a beautiful baby boy—who began to cry. Human compassion, a gift of God, welled in her as she realized it was the baby of a Hebrew. She adopted the baby for herself and gave him an Egyptian name—*Moses*—a form of the verb *to draw out* because she had drawn him from the water. (Exodus 2:5-10)

Laying her infant son in the tiny boat was a supreme act of faith. There is no record in the Bible that God spoke or directed the mother to take this step. Perhaps the decision was initially an act of calculation. She could not hide her son forever, and the present course meant only delaying inevitable death. Still, there was no way to know how the story would end. Cruel and depraved eyes might spot the basket and follow Pharaoh's death order. Perhaps no one would spot the basket, and the child would slowly die of starvation or exposure.

It is a fitting picture of life for all of us. What do we truly know when entering the boat that promises life? We know that the old life holds no promise, except a fearful expectancy of death without hope. The boat may appear flimsy and uncertain, but what is the alternative?

The Bible records that crowds followed Jesus throughout His earthly ministry. They were awed by healings, and eagerly sought the bread and fish miraculously multiplied, but greater demands would come. When Jesus began teaching about the cost of following him, things changed quickly. There was talk of *eating His flesh, and drinking His blood*, and the people responded: "*This is a hard saying: who can understand it?*" (John 6: 52-60 NKJV) Even the disciples were thrown by such difficult words. As if this was not difficult enough, Jesus added "There are some of you who do not believe... Therefore I have said to you that no one can come to Me unless it has been granted to him by my Father." (John 6:64-65 NKJV) Following this, the scripture records that many of His disciples turned away and no longer followed Him. In so tragic a moment, Jesus turned to the twelve apostles, His closest followers, and asked "Do you also want to go away?" (John 6:67 NKJV)

It was Peter who spoke for them all: "Lord, to whom shall we go? You have the words of eternal life." (John 6:68 NKJV) The same Peter who had climbed from so many earthly boats saw clearly now. What other option could there possibly be? What could the world offer any longer to match this promise? Through the dim light of this world, the way in front was uncertain—but the old ways had no promise at all. Whatever the figurative boat was before them, they would climb in with Jesus.

The Conclusion

The actions of Moses' mother were more than desperate steps by a frightened mother. Leaving her baby, as she did, was a supreme act of faith and trust in God. It was a step to preserve life rather than waiting for the inevitable detection that brought certain death. It was also a selfless act that valued the life of her baby above her own. Even if she would lose the joy of raising her son, she opted for what was best for him and his best chance of life. It was a heartbreaking act of sacrifice and supreme love. She had surrendered his life in order to save it, while trusting that nothing could harm her child unless God permitted it.

Life constantly brings us such challenges and decisions that can only be met by faith in God. Sometimes that faith compels us to leave a boat we should never have entered. On some occasions, it will bid us to enter a boat, trusting fully in the love of a gracious God and Savior.

What are the consequences of failing to enter a boat of deliverance? Imagine having been on the beaches of France during the battle of Dunkirk, with German artillery blazing in the background and the *Luftwaffe's* planes strafing and bombing the narrow beaches. Imagine how intensely you would have wanted to enter one of the boats coming to the shore, knowing it held the promise of your deliverance. With each wave of boats arriving, you would watch eagerly, knowing you were getting closer to your turn. Finally, the call and waving arms from the water; imagine the elation when your boat arrived! What once seemed like certain death or imprisonment was turned with the arrival of a boat.

There is the same joy and elation for all who understand and appropriate God's plan for deliverance. Those who have trusted in the saving work of Jesus Christ experience the mysterious love and peace that come from surrender to God. Jesus once said that those who seek to save or keep there lives will lose them, while the one who loses his life *for Christ's sake* will find it. (Matthew 10:39) It is the paradoxical kingdom of God, where the last are first, the weak are strong, and where the one who is greatest is servant to all.

Entering into that voyage of faith is the greatest purpose in any life. And those who enter the boat of deliverance are set free from the fate that sin and separation from God brings. Those who enter this boat discover the greatest truth of life—namely, that the Son of Man came to seek and save those who are lost. It is the great boat of eternal life and peace with God for those who come aboard. If you are not already on board, call out today to the God who loves you more than you can know or imagine, and who bids you to enter His boat of deliverance.

ENDNOTES

Chapter One

[1] *Blind Man's Bluff,* Sherry Sontag and Christopher Drew, Perennial Publishers, 2000, at p. 112
[2] Dunmore, Spencer Lost Subs (2002), Madison Press Books at page 157
[3] *Excerpted from:* The New York Times on the Web, 26Oct00, Associated Press
[4] Account taken from "From This Verse," Robert J. Morgan, Pub. Thomas Nelson, 1998 at January, 23 entry.

Chapter Two

[1] The New International Encyclopedia of Bible Words, Zondervan, 1998 at p. 334.
[2] *Surprised By Joy* at p. 226

Chapter Four

[1] According to other sources, there was probably far more than twice the human capacity.
[2] Readers interested in reading further accounts of the Sultana are recommended to Walker's account published under "Bits of Blue and Gray" in 2007.

Chapter Five

[1]"Treasure Trove in Gaspé and the Baie des Chaleur", published by Quebec Telegraph Print Co, 1919. The account from which this is drawn was posted by G.R. Bosse in 1998

Chapter Six

[1] The keel is a structural piece of the hull, usually attached at a right angle, which aids in stability.

[2] http://www.encyclopedia-titanica.org/andrea-doria-the-sinking-of-the-unsinkable.html

[3] Publius Flavius Vegetius, *Military Institutions of the Romans* at 4.39

[4] "Soundings" were taken by dropping a weighted rope to the sea floor. As the distance decreased sailors could determine that a boat was nearing land.

Chapter Eight

[1]Eyewitness to History.com: http://www.eyewitnesstohistory.com/dunkirk.htm